Cambridge Ele

Elements in Public and Nonprofi
edited by
Andrew Whitford
University of Georgia
Robert Christensen
Brigham Young University

SHARED MEASURES

Collective Performance Data Use in Collaborations

Alexander Kroll
Florida International University

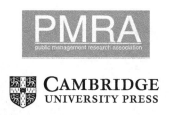

CAMBRIDGE
UNIVERSITY PRESS

CAMBRIDGE
UNIVERSITY PRESS

University Printing House, Cambridge CB2 8BS, United Kingdom

One Liberty Plaza, 20th Floor, New York, NY 10006, USA

477 Williamstown Road, Port Melbourne, VIC 3207, Australia

314–321, 3rd Floor, Plot 3, Splendor Forum, Jasola District Centre, New Delhi – 110025, India

103 Penang Road, #05–06/07, Visioncrest Commercial, Singapore 238467

Cambridge University Press is part of the University of Cambridge.

It furthers the University's mission by disseminating knowledge in the pursuit of education, learning, and research at the highest international levels of excellence.

www.cambridge.org
Information on this title: www.cambridge.org/9781108927611
DOI: 10.1017/9781108933025

© Alexander Kroll 2022

First published 2022

A catalogue record for this publication is available from the British Library.

ISBN 978-1-108-92761-1 Paperback
ISSN 2515-4303 (online)
ISSN 2515-429X (print)

Shared Measures

Collective Performance Data Use in Collaborations

Elements in Public and Nonprofit Administration

DOI: 10.1017/9781108933025
First published online: February 2022

Alexander Kroll
Florida International University

Author for correspondence: Alexander Kroll, akroll@fiu.edu

Abstract: Traditionally, performance metrics and data have been used to hold organizations accountable. But public service provision is not merely hierarchical anymore. Increasingly, we see partnerships among government agencies, private or nonprofit organizations, and civil society groups. Such collaborations may also use goals, measures, and data to manage group efforts; however, the application of performance practices here will likely follow a different logic. This Element introduces the concepts of "shared measures" and "collective data use" to add collaborative, relational elements to existing performance management theory. It draws on a case study of collaboratives in North Carolina that were established to develop community responses to the opioid epidemic. To explain the use of shared performance measures and data within these collaboratives, this Element studies the role of factors such as group composition, participatory structures, social relationships, distributed leadership, group culture, and value congruence.

Keywords: performance management, performance information use, collaborative governance, group decision-making, opioid epidemic

ISBNs: 9781108927611 (PB), 9781108933025 (OC)
ISSNs: 2515-4303 (online), 2515-429X (print)

Contents

1 Introduction

Most research on performance measures begins with the distinction between principals and agents. It assumes that agents act opportunistically, which is why principals need measures and data to monitor task implementation. Public service provision is known for its many levels of principal–agent relationships: within and across government organizations as well as built into external contracts and grants. This is the environment from which most research on performance systems has grown. It includes work concerned with measurement questions, followed by research on data use and nonuse in decision-making, and the link between performance management and organizational improvements. Scholarship has also examined dysfunctions, contradictions, and behavioral biases related to performance management (e.g., Ammons, 2020; Gerrish, 2016; James et al., 2020; Kroll, 2015a).

Most performance systems are set up within the boundaries of one organization's or jurisdiction's responsibilities to manage subagencies, contractors, or employees. However, effective public service provision increasingly requires independent organizations (across sectors) to work together. Such collaborations are voluntary, and they occur outside of the traditionally hierarchical structure of the bureaucracy. They can involve organizations from different levels of government, nonprofit organizations as well as civic and community groups, particularly if the issues they try to address are complex and cannot simply be fixed via government intervention or regulation (Bryson et al., 2015; Emerson & Nabatchi, 2015a; Isett et al., 2011).

Examples of collaborations include initiatives dealing with traffic congestion in urban areas, mitigating alcohol consumption in the amateur sports community, or addressing environmental watershed issues (Douglas & Ansell, 2021; Imperial, 2004; Page et al., 2015). In other instances, collaborative governance regimes help coordinate efforts among otherwise independent government agencies or departments. One such case is the collaboration between the U.S. Border Patrol and the Forest Service to better operate a segment of the Mexico–U.S. border (Emerson & Nabatchi, 2015b). Another example includes collaborations among agencies within the federal government using cross-agency priority goals (Choi & Moynihan, 2019).

The collaborations mentioned earlier vary greatly regarding their policy area and context, but they share a commonality. The researchers studying these cases make suggestions on how to adapt performance regimes to the specific needs of collaborative settings. I will review the specific ideas proposed in these pieces, and in other relevant work, in more detail later. Taken together, however, they all point to the following broader questions: How do we conceptualize "performance" in collaboratives that consist of diverse actors with different interests and objectives? How can we use *shared* performance measures to manage for results in the absence of hierarchical and principal–agent relationships? What can we do to facilitate the collective use of shared measures and data in collaborative decision-making?

1.1 Shared Measures

When referring to shared measures, I use them as an umbrella concept that incorporates shared goals, indicators, and data. While this is an expansive use of the term *measure*, it is also intuitive and understood by government practitioners. Managing with performance measures implies that such measures are linked to goals and that data will be collected based on these measures. In that sense, "shared measures" is short for an entire set of shared performance management practices.

Shared measures have at least one similarity with more conventional performance metrics: they are the result of a systematic and routine management effort. That is, performance feedback is generated based on quantitative indicators that are supposed to capture the achievement of a predefined objective (Ammons, 2020; Hatry, 2006). Hence, shared measures – and performance metrics more generally – are different from all types of non-routine feedback (Kroll, 2013). The latter includes performance information that is ad hoc, episodic, verbal, and often not actively pursued but passively received via several sources (Mintzberg, 1975; Olsen, 2017; Tantardini, 2019).

What makes shared measures different from other routine performance practices is their use in the context of collaborative governance regimes. Such regimes have been characterized as "processes or structures ... that engage people constructively across the boundaries of public agencies, levels of government, and/or the public, private and civic spheres in order to carry out a public purpose" (Emerson et al., 2012, p. 2). In this context then, I employ the following definition: *Shared measures are goals, indicators, and data that were agreed upon by a collaborative, span across organizational boundaries, and capture quantifiable changes in output or outcome performance for which the collaborative is jointly responsible.* As such, it is not the metric that makes a shared measure different from a conventional performance indicator, but the collaborative processes through which the metric is selected, defined, and used. Of course, my definition is that of an ideal type, acknowledging that, even in collaborative settings, some performance practices may be "more shared" than in others.

Shared measures are agreed upon by a collaborative. In the absence of a hierarchy, goals and measures are not set by a principal and then worked toward by an agent. Instead, the members of the collaborative need to identify and agree upon goals, measures, and data sources as the result of a group effort. *Shared measures span across organizational boundaries.* The rationale behind forming collaborations is commonly that a single organization is unable to solve a complex problem without other groups or agencies cooperating. If the production of outputs or the improvement of outcomes requires multiple actors to work together, then the key performance measures need to reflect this collective effort. *Shared measures capture changes in performance for which the collaborative is jointly responsible.* Members of collaboratives are the ones defining goals and measure as well as implementing actions to achieve these goals. Often, there is no external overseeing body whose purpose is to monitor the collaboration members and hold them accountable. Hence, the collaborative as a whole needs to take on responsibility for performance improvements (or a lack thereof) and self-manage.

There are performance practices that involve collaboration but do not necessarily fall under my definition. For instance, collaborative performance summits may not necessarily use shared measures (Douglas & Ansell, 2021). While summit attendees represent a diverse set of organizations that work toward the same goal, each organization may use its own separate performance system in lieu of shared measures. This is particularly true if the summit members' systems are actor-centric as opposed to network-centric (Douglas & Ansell, 2021, p. 953). In such cases, performance practices would not be jointly designed, and they would lack shared responsibilities. So, while performance summits certainly have collaborative elements, such as boundary-spanning lesson learning, they do not necessarily make use of shared measures.

PerformanceStat systems, such as CompStat or CitiStat, most likely do not use shared measures. While *Stat* meetings bring together different actors from various departments and sometimes even organizations, they miss the "sharing part" that is supposed to occur among partners who work together on equal terms. In fact, most Stat approaches are very hierarchical with a clear principal–agent structure, where top-level leaders use measures and data to hold middle managers accountable for changes in their unit's performance (Behn, 2014; Pasha et al., 2021). While PerformanceStat approaches can vary in terms of their aggressiveness, they rarely mirror the idea of a horizontally structured and voluntarily formed collaborative in which partners have equal say regarding the design and use of shared measures. In its more aggressive configuration, Stat puts managers in the "hot seat," where they are quizzed or even "cross-examined" about the performance deficits of their individual units.

Learning forums may use shared measures, but they often do not. First and foremost, learning forums tend to coordinate activities within one agency rather than across several organizations or groups (James et al., 2020; Moynihan, 2008). They facilitate a dialogue among actors from different hierarchical levels, but whether such an approach is truly collaborative may vary across organizations. Another feature that is often missing is that learning forums focus on the use and sensemaking of existing systems rather than jointly developing shared performance practices. As such, learning forums can serve as a vehicle for the use of shared measures; however, in practice, they rarely do.

In this subsection, I have provided a definition of the term shared measures, which I hoped to be broad and inclusive. I also reviewed a few popular concepts and approaches, some of which lend themselves to the application of shared measures. However, not every performance system that features one or more collaborative element(s) fits under the shared measures label. This distinction is important because "shared measures theory" may only apply to cases where collaboration members are truly able to share in the development and use of performance practices.

1.2 Approach of This Element

1.2.1 Argument

Collaborations should make use of performance practices. And they do, as the previous examples illustrate. As such, the general logic behind the performance management principle will likely also apply to collaborations. Defining goals and using measures and data to track achievements may help groups to close performance gaps and yield improvements. At the same time, adoptions of performance approaches should be informed by the experiences made within the traditional agency setting. This includes awareness of misleading assumptions about rationality and objectivity as well as the unintended consequences of overly rigid systems that may, in fact, incentivize dysfunctional responses and behaviors (Heinrich & Marschke, 2010; Kroll, 2015a; Moynihan, 2009).

However, one must be cautious with simplistic transfers of "systems" from the traditional agency to the collaboration context. This is mostly because important administrative routines featured in public organizations are largely absent in collaborative arrangements. Think, for example, of performance contracts or bargains, reporting requirements, and traditional top-down monitoring that are present in most traditional performance systems but almost impossible to recreate (and probably unwanted) in horizontally configured collaborations. Hence, some of the content of performance management could be adapted to collaborative settings (definitions of performance, requirements for high-quality measures, etc.), whereas related processes, such as *how to* develop measures or facilitate the use of data, need to be comprehensively revised.

I argue that the collective use of performance information in collaborations is different from organization-centered use, which I categorize as being either institutionalized or discretionary. Both of these uses are located within the public sector hierarchy and their focus is on managing individuals or organizations. Data use is institutionalized if it is regulated by formal requirements or informal norms. The part of use that cannot be regulated – which is cognitive and shaped by individual judgment – I label as "discretionary." Collective use is different, in that it occurs within multi-organizational networks and its reference point is the group level. It refers to data use that is negotiated among equal partners, and performance information here likely fits my ideal-type definition of shared measures.

While collective use is different from the other two modes, some of what we have learned about institutionalized and discretionary use can be adapted to the "collaboration case." For example, lessons from interactive dialogue theory may travel well across contexts. Yet, explaining collective use means shifting away from agency theory, which emphasizes self-interest-driven incentivization, and better-involving stewardship approaches, which are built around the ideas of aligning goals and values. To understand the use of performance data, and shared measures in particular, in collaborations more comprehensively, I argue that it is necessary to turn to relational theoretical perspectives and approaches.

While relational theory has been applied to model relationships among organizations, it has been largely disregarded in the performance information use literature, which is mostly focused on formal system requirements, organizational features, or the individual data user. In this Element, I examine six relational perspectives and, hence, take a closer look at the role of group composition, egalitarian structures, social relationships, distributed leadership, group culture, and value congruence. Overall, studying the collective use of shared measures requires taking performance management research into a new, mostly unexplored direction since existing theories will need to be revised and expanded, given the unique characteristics of the collaboration context.

1.2.2 Research Design

To examine the argument outlined earlier, the Element employs what others have called an instrumental or explanatory cases study (Stake, 1995; Yin, 2017). The case will be used to understand and explain causal relationships, specifically those between the collective use of shared measures and its potential antecedents. The case-study approach has been employed as it allows an in-depth inquiry into a complex phenomenon and is particularly useful if the boundaries between the phenomenon and its context are blurry (Yin, 2017). I use the case study to illustrate the extent to which the explanations of shared measures use vary from the use of performance metrics in traditional, hierarchical settings as documented in the extant literature. Furthermore, I am concerned with identifying more and less influential explanatory variables. Generalizations will be analytic rather than following the paradigm of sample-to-population inferences.

My case study is on opioid-response collaborations in North Carolina (2019–2020). Across the United States, the opioid epidemic poses a major governance and public health challenge. Between 1999 and 2019, about 500,000 people died from an overdose involving prescription and illicit opioids (CDC, 2021a). Recently, the COVID-19 pandemic seemed to have supercharged a death spike related to drug and opioid overdoses (Katz & Sanger-Katz, 2021). What started out with the overprescription of painkillers turned into a multifaceted "wicked problem" (Lee, 2018) that involves abuse, addiction, mental disorders, criminalization, and illicit drugs as well as social and economic hardship. In such a context, the case study is concerned with how communities in the state of North Carolina responded to the epidemic. A context factor that these communities share is that their efforts are organized via collaborations that involve local government agencies, nonprofit actors, and civil society.

The main reason for selecting this case is that it offers a de facto natural quasi-experiment that directly maps onto this Element's main research question. The School of Government (SOG) at the University of North Carolina (UNC) at Chapel Hill set up a program to help communities within the state address the opioid epidemic locally (Nelson, 2021; SOG, 2021). As a part of that program, ten community collaboratives received training regarding the management of such groups, including training on the use of shared measures. This then created the rare opportunity to observe how the use of shared performance practices played out across ten newly formed collaboratives that all received the same training, thereby allowing the examination of the impact of different group dynamics and configurations on such practices.[1]

---

[1] I served as one of the instructors providing SOG's training "treatment." Again, this treatment was given to all ten groups, and the interesting question was to study whether – and why – groups responded differently to the input. My research, despite my involvement in delivering the treatment, does not qualify as action research since the study participants did not take on the role of researchers, and the research interest was not tailored to answering a practical question unique to the case (Zhang et al., 2015).

The study applies an embedded single-case study design (Yin, 2017). The first unit of analysis is the "North Carolina case" or, more specifically, statewide patterns in responding to the epidemic that hold across community collaboratives. At this level, I draw most of my inferences in an attempt to identify generalizable relationships; important context factors specific to the state and the SOG program are located here as well. I organize findings at this macro level by variables of interest (rather than sites) and – where helpful – pool data across groups. The second unit of analysis consists of the ten community collaboratives. Most of my data collection instruments employ the community level as their point of reference. Furthermore, at this level, I will contrast findings across two divergent community groups in more detail.

As conducting a case study allows the use of mixed methods (Yin, 2006), in order to strengthen the validity of the findings, I triangulate (a) methods, (b) data sources, and (c) the times of data collection. Regarding the methods, I use surveys, interviews, focus groups, and document reviews. With respect to data sources, my qualitative instruments collect data from "key players" (core group members and trainers[2]), whereas the quantitative surveys cast a much wider net. Table 1 shows which instruments were used at what point in time for the purpose of data collection.

All interviews were semi-structured and followed an open-ended question route (each took about forty-five minutes). In total, I conducted fifteen interviews (including those with trainers). The number of interviews was sufficient to gain rich descriptions of the perceptions of a selected few, but not large enough for more extensive text analysis. Rather, I wrote summaries of the

Table 1 Data collection instruments

Date	Instrument	N
2019/03	Main Survey (Part 1)	~145
2019/09	One-Page Survey (Forum 3)	48
2019/11	Review of Ten Performance Plans	–
2019/11	Focus Groups/Interviews with Ten Groups	10*
2020/02–07	Interviews with Trainers and Follow-Ups	5
2020/08	Main Survey (Part 2)	~120

Note: * Each of these focus groups/interviews was conducted with 1–4 individuals.

---

[2] Faculty and staff who worked on an interdisciplinary team that helped support and provide training and resources to the groups.

recorded material and contrasted major similarities and differences across groups. The purpose of the interviews was to collect background information about the groups and their work products, while being aware that the perspective of most interviewees was that of the "in-group member." For the document analysis, I reviewed each group's performance plans, including vision documents, action plans, and performance indicator sheets.

The surveys allowed me to better quantify some of the findings and reach out to a larger sample of group members. The main surveys were administered at the beginning and end of the project, and they targeted the full population of group members. Providing reliable response rates is difficult because the surveys were sent to all individuals who had given their contact information to one of the coordinators of a collaborative. However, some of these individuals only attended one meeting, left the group after a few meetings, or they were on the contact list by mistake. In such cases, said individuals should be considered as falsely included in the sampling frame rather than being nonrespondents. An additional survey was distributed during one of the forums where about fifty representatives of all groups came together to meet with the SOG team and trainers.

The remainder of the Element is organized to position my arguments within the extant literature (Section 2), propose a set of causal mechanisms (Section 3), conduct an empirical case study (Section 4), and draw out conclusions for theory and practice (Section 5).

2 Institutionalized, Discretionary, and Collective Data Use

This section categorizes the existing performance management literature into the streams of institutionalized and discretionary data use. This is done to differentiate these two perspectives, which were both established in the context of the public-sector hierarchy, from collective use that I associate with collaborations. To that end, this section provides conceptualizations of all three frames in which data use occurs. It synthesizes theories and empirical work to illustrate similarities and differences across these frames and identify the nature of, and mechanisms behind, collective use. However, I begin with a brief review of what the collaboration literature says about performance measures.

2.1 Perspectives on Performance Measures in Collaboration Research

Collaboration research incorporates the topics of performance and performance management, with an emphasis on questions of accountability (Agranoff, 2007). Bryson and colleagues (2006) consider accountability to be "a particularly complex issue for collaborations because it is not often clear whom the collaborative is accountable to and for what" (p. 51). Kettl (2006) points to the same problem – "if everyone is in charge, is anyone in charge?" (p. 17) – and McGuire (2013) identifies creating accountability as one of the core competencies for the purpose of effectively managing networks. While most people would agree that addressing accountability-related questions remains a significant challenge for collaborations, it is noteworthy that research (mostly produced outside of the collaboration realm) has shown that accountability is only one out of many purposes for which performance data and systems could be used (Kroll, 2015a; Moynihan, 2009; Van Dooren et al., 2015). In that sense then, performance data – or more specifically shared measures – could add a great deal of value for managing collaborations if used for alternative purposes, including to evaluate, control, budget, motivate, promote, celebrate, learn, and improve (Behn, 2003).

Other work is concerned with the conceptualization of what performance means for cross-organization collaborations. For instance, Emerson and Nabatchi (2015b) argue that for a collaborative regime to be considered effective, it needs to satisfy stakeholders with different interests and priorities across several potential performance dimensions. Page and colleagues (2015) use a public-value perspective to develop a framework that not only draws on widely known subdimensions of performance (efficiency, effectiveness, equity) but also incorporates novel concepts such as capacity building. Moynihan and colleagues (2011) point to the fact that defining performance and selecting shared measures can be difficult in collaborations because authority is dispersed, and principal–agent roles are blurred. Along these lines, performance practices can help better manage collaborations (Imperial, 2004), but collaborators have a variety of implementation options to choose from (Douglas & Ansell, 2021), and poor adaptations to the collaborative context can be harmful as well (Denhardt & Aristigueta, 2008).

Most research so far has given little attention to the theme that is the focus of this Element: understanding differences in the use of shared measures for group decision-making. Page (2004) labels such behavior as managing for results, and he speaks more specifically of "the capacity to use data about results strategically to assess progress and to improve policies and operations in the future" (p. 593). Yet, we find little scholarship on the empirical underpinnings of shared measures use. One exception is a study by Choi and Moynihan (2019), wherein they examine interagency collaborations in the U.S. federal government and, among other things, emphasize the adverse effects between existing agency-focused systems and collaborative performance management efforts.

This Element is about the use of performance data for decision-making or, more specifically, the collective use of shared measures for managing collaborations. One prominently featured typology that clarifies the term "data use" is known as Moynihan's (2009) four Ps: purposeful, passive, political, and perverse use. In a nutshell, purposeful use is the type that is normatively desired and often associated with improvements, learning, and better-informed management. Passive use is about complying with data reporting requirements. Political use refers to employing data as ammunition in negotiations. Finally, perverse use captures dysfunctional behaviors such as data manipulation and gaming. Most research on these types of use has been conducted within the traditional public-sector hierarchy (for an overview, see Kroll, 2015a; Moynihan & Pandey, 2010).

To conceptualize data use in a collaborative setting, I take a step back from purposes of use and instead theorize "use" based on different organizational structures in which it is embedded. I begin with a hierarchical perspective that distinguishes between institutionalized and discretionary use. I then shed light on the collaborative environment that features collective use. The purpose behind this categorization is to articulate the idea of collective use by contrasting it against the two more conventional modes. While my typology of the three modes of use is novel, I will show that a large amount of the existing empirical literature fits under the umbrella that these three ideal types provide. In fact, I will synthesize and connect theories and empirics related to institutionalized and discretionary use to better substantiate our understanding of collective use.

2.2 Modes of Data Use: Institutionalized, Discretionary, and Collective

Conceptualizations such as the four Ps define performance information use by the varying purposes they serve. My starting point here is different, in that I distinguish modes of use based on the organizational frame in which they occur. Such a frame can be explicit or implicit. In an explicit frame, use is institutionalized via formal or informal norms, while in an implicit frame, use tends to be discretionary. The explicit frame captures the part of use that is organized through the establishment of structures, rules, and values that configure the relationships among actors or agencies. In contrast, the implicit frame describes the part of use that is more internal and rather difficult to structure and regulate. The explicit-implicit distinction makes few normative assumptions. Essentially, all purposes of use that the four Ps feature could occur under either the explicit or implicit frame.

A widely shared assumption is that performance information use in the public sector occurs within a hierarchical setting, including contracts with nonprofit actors or private companies (Brown et al., 2006; Moynihan, 2008; Schillemans & Bjurstrøm, 2019). Often, public organizations take on roles as both principals and agents. That is, they report to higher-level organizations while also overseeing lower-level subagencies or contractors. Figure 1 illustrates such a scenario. We can read this figure from the point of view of organization three (O3 for short). Here, O3 reports to O1, but it also manages O5 and O6. In this context, an explicit performance frame may be utilized to institutionalize expectations about O3's data use for both its roles as a principal and as an agent.

When referring to "institutions," I adopt North's (2008) definition of "rules of the game – both formal rules and informal norms and their enforcement characteristics" (p. 22). While formal rules (laws, property rights, and regulations) can be enforced legally, informal norms (taboos, customs, traditions, and codes of conduct) tend to be enforced by peers (Hodgson, 2006; North, 1991). Hence, when theorizing about institutionalized use, I refer to expectations about behavior that are either formally regulated or informally expressed via social structures. Along these lines, in Figure 1, O3 is either coercively or normatively animated to use data in order to report on its performance to O1 and manage and control O5 and O6.

Not all use can be institutionalized (Kroll, 2015a; Moynihan, 2009; Moynihan & Pandey, 2010). In fact, almost every data use behavior can be distinguished into a part that is programmable and a residual part that remains discretionary. Keeping this in mind, let us take another look at the four Ps. Purposeful behavior, such as using performance data to motivate employees, can be made explicit to some extent. For instance, a formal appraisal system can be developed that defines objectives, measures, and rewards. Explicit informal norms may shape the process as well ("usually, everyone gets a 4 or 5 … "). However, there will still be important parts of the review process that are discretionary, such as the interpretation of performance criteria, the tone of

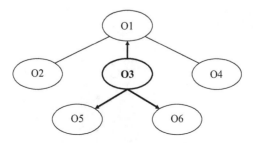

Figure 1 Institutionalized use

the conversation, the incorporation of context information, or the decision on the final rating and how this will be linked motivational practices not specified in the formal reward structure.

The same holds true for other types of data use. Passive use is probably the type that can be regulated the most through formalized reporting requirements and the definition of measures. Still, managers have the discretion to decide which data they select and how they present them; and behavioral research has documented that visualization choices and accompanying narratives can affect interpretations significantly (for an overview, see James et al., 2020). Political and more symbolic uses are often integrated in established political negotiation and communication routines (Van Dooren & Van de Walle, 2008). However, it is up to a manager's discretion whether she uses a high or a low performance score to advocate for more resources (to be rewarded for excellence as opposed to getting support for dealing with difficult tasks), and which context information she pairs the data with. Although rarely intended formally, perverse use often results from institutionalized mis-specified reward structures. Still, managers tend to respond differently to the same incentive system (Bohte & Meier, 2000; Kroll & Vogel, 2021), suggesting that there are additional implicit factors that matter even to dysfunctional behaviors.

Figure 2 illustrates discretionary use under an implicit performance frame. Organizations (again, let us read this from O3's view) are embedded in a hierarchical system. However, while expectations about data use regarding O3's interactions with other units can be institutionalized, a significant part of performance information use is likely to occur within O3's zone of discretion (the area shaded in grey). In this area, under the implicit frame, it is difficult to regulate or mandate behaviors, especially more so if they are internal and cognitive or involve interpretation, argumentation, and professional judgment. As Dermer and Lucas (1986) argue in "The Illusion of Managerial Control," discretion increases as it becomes more difficult to specify expectations, engage in measurement, attribute causality, and intervene in a functional way.

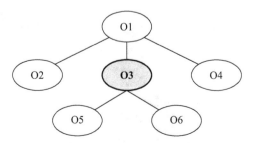

Figure 2 Discretionary use

The idea behind the institutionalized-discretionary use distinction is not to develop new behavioral measures or survey items. Rather, this distinction provides a framework in which data use (such as the behaviors captured via the four Ps) occurs, thereby, allowing us to theorize a broader typology of ideal type-like use contexts. It is also noteworthy that the same use behavior may be categorized differently based on the explicit or implicit frame in which it is situated. For example, using performance information to motivate employees may be more on the institutionalized side if there is a formal appraisal system in place that the manager follows closely. In a different organization, the same behavior can be more discretionary in the absence of a formal or informal process. This leaves the manager in a position to rely more fully on her own sensemaking when it comes to evaluating achievements based on quantifiable evidence.

While use is more likely to be institutionalized *between* organizations and discretionary *within* the organization, a rigid external-internal dichotomy would be an over-simplification. Instead, the model portrayed in Figure 2 could be cascaded down throughout the organizational hierarchy. In that sense, O3 could also be a department within an organization or a middle manager. Similar to the point I made before, some portion of the department's or manager's data use could likely be institutionalized, while a residual part would remain discretionary. However, most literature that theorizes about performance, contracts, and relations employed the organization as their unit of analysis (e.g., Amirkhanyan et al., 2012; Bjurstrøm, 2019; Han, 2020). To be consistent with this previous work, I conceptualize O3 here as a semi-independent but interconnected organization and not as a department, team, or individual within an organization.

How does the institutionalized-discretionary use distinction fit within existing research? There is a large amount of work that maps onto either of these ideal types, although this work has rarely been directly related to (or contrasted with) each other. On one hand, research with a focus on accountability issues has been concerned with the role of institutions, including formal performance practices, in shaping principal–agent relations in the public sector (e.g., Askim et al., 2019; Lu, 2016; Van Slyke, 2007). On the other hand, management-oriented research operationalized the use of performance information as autonomous behavior, which is driven by managerial, organizational, and context factors that are largely located outside of the institutional bargain over objectives and incentives (e.g., Kroll, 2015a; Moynihan & Pandey, 2010; Webeck & Nicholson-Crotty, 2020). I will further synthesize these literatures below.

Contrasting my typology with the one developed in a conceptual paper by Jakobsen and colleagues (2018) may further help position it within the extant literature. Jakobsen and colleagues argue that there are two types of perform-ance regimes: those focused on external accountability and those focused on internal learning. The accountability regime is based on external goals and high-powered incentives. The learning regime provides more goal autonomy, incen-tives are aimed at norms and values, and external relations are framed as a dialogue. Overall, this perspective is compatible with the one I presented earlier. It conceptualizes data use within the public sector hierarchy, and its external-internal distinction maps onto my typology of institutionalized and discretionary behaviors.

However, there are also several differences between the two approaches. First, my framework accounts for the fact that a fair amount of use can be formally institutionalized even within the organization, which is why I do not focus as much on the inside-outside distinction. Second, while Jakobsen and colleagues (2018) persuasively argue that purposeful learning is more likely to occur in the "internal" regime, my typology makes no such normative assump-tions. Rather, I posit that institutionalized and discretionary use can be purpose-ful, political, passive, as well as perverse. Third, Jakobsen and colleagues (2018) conceptualize data use from the perspective of the agent in a hierarchical system, whereas my typology acknowledges that many public organizations are both principals and agents. Therefore, the same performance system used to hold an organization accountable (such as O3 in Figure 1) could be used by that very same organization to manage its subagencies. Finally, while I have so far mostly discussed institutionalized and discretionary uses, my typology includes a third mode to which most other research has only given little attention: collective use.

Here, I provide an initial explanation of collective use by contrasting this mode with the ones discussed earlier (see also Table 2). Institutional and discretionary use are both based on the assumption that managers and agencies are located within the hierarchical structure of the public sector. However, we find increasing evidence that important public service functions are delivered through collaborations of actors and organizations whose interactions can be characterized as largely voluntary and lateral (Choi & Moynihan, 2019; Douglas & Ansell, 2021; Emerson & Nabatchi, 2015b; Imperial, 2004; Page et al., 2015).

There are at least two more attributes that the institutionalized and discre-tionary modes have in common: use is conceptualized as individual or organ-izational behavior, and performance measures and data are defined or collected within the boundaries of the organization (e.g., Ammons, 2020; Kroll, 2015a; Moynihan & Pandey, 2010). I argue that such a view is incomplete. It, for the most part, disregards one alternative mode: collective use. The latter refers to

Table 2 Modes of performance data use

	Institutionalized	Discretionary	Collective
Definition	Refers to the portion of performance data use that is regulated by systems or norms.	Refers to the portion of performance data use that is cognitive and shaped by individual judgment.	Refers to the portion of performance data use that is negotiated among equal partners.
Visualization			
Organizational frame	Expectations for data use are explicitly articulated via formal or informal performance bargains.	Expectations for data use remain implicit, but use can be fostered via factors that are often located outside of performance bargains.	Expectations for data use are established via ongoing dialogue. Use is discretionary but can be loosely institutionalized.
Surrounding structure	Use is embedded in public sector hierarchy.	Use is embedded in public sector hierarchy.	Use is embedded in public sector networks.
Reference point	Individual or single organization	Individual or single organization	Group or multiple organizations
Impetus	Addressing an extrinsically framed problem.	Addressing an intrinsically framed problem.	Addressing an intrinsically framed problem.
Measures and data	Performance measures and data defined or collected within the boundaries of the organization.	Performance measures and data defined or collected within the boundaries of the organization.	Shared measures and data defined by a collaborative, which span across organizational boundaries.

Note: Cells shaded in grey indicate areas in which the marked modes overlap.

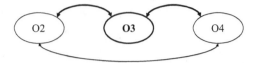

Figure 3 Collective use

the portion of performance data use that is negotiated among equal partners. It occurs outside of the hierarchy and is embedded in public sector networks. As shown in Figure 3, data are used jointly through voluntary, reciprocal, and lateral interactions among O2, O3, and O4.

The reference point for collective use is a group of actors or the representatives of multiple organizations. Rather than being organization-centered, collective use is based on shared measures and data defined by a collaborative, which spans across organizational boundaries. Douglas and Ansell (2021) rightly point out that, even in a collaborative setting, data use can be more or less network centric. That is, rather than being shared, measurement and data use can still be individualized and dominated by organization-centric metrics. My understanding is that collective use, at least when conceptualized as an ideal type, needs to draw on network-centric shared measures and practices. Such measures will not only help specify and make sense of the collaborative's joint purpose, but they can also create social pressure and transparency in the absence of a hierarchy ensuring all members contribute to the achievement of collective goals (Imperial, 2004).

But we also see similarities with the other two modes of use. Much like the discretionary approach, problems to be addressed using collective performance practices tend to be intrinsically framed. Further, collective use is discretionary to the extent that it is difficult to mandate, and its outcomes are difficult to predict. At the same time, collective use may be loosely institutionalized via norms and values that grow out of ongoing social interactions among collaboration partners. It is along these lines that I argue that some of the research on institutionalized and discretionary use can help us better conceptualize the third, mostly understudied, mode of collective use. In the following subsections, I will review and synthesize additional empirical literature to further substantiate all three modes of use and showcase their distinctions and interconnections, with the purpose in mind to develop a more nuanced understanding of collective use.

2.3 Theories of Institutionalized Use

In this subsection, I synthesize three theories that have been utilized in performance management research to conceptualize and understand institutionalized use among actors or organizations. This includes two approaches that are largely considered as alternative schools of thought – agency theory (2.3.1) and stewardship theory (2.3.3) – with the interactive dialogue model (2.3.2) sandwiched in-between.

2.3.1 Agency Theory

According to agency theory, principals delegate tasks to agents because of the former's lack of expertise or capacity. Both principals and agents are self-interested, and their interests rarely align naturally. As such, the relationship between principal and agent is metaphorically understood as a contract. Since agents know more about the delegated task, they tend to exploit information asymmetries for their own benefit. To mitigate the agency problem, principals establish information and performance systems to monitor agents (Jensen & Meckling, 1976; Schillemans & Bjurstrøm, 2019; Van Slyke, 2007). Contracts need to be focused on outcomes, as opposed to behaviors, if causalities behind outcomes are widely understood, and outcomes can be accurately measured, or if it is difficult to specify agent behavior (Eisenhardt, 1989; for extensions, see Miller, 2005).

Agency theory calls for formal performance agreements between principals and agents. On the part of the principal, such agreements institutionalize performance data use for the purpose of controlling and monitoring agents, possibly via routines of data review. On the part of the agent, data use is institutionalized for compliance with reporting requirements. At the same time, however, expectations of use can be institutionalized, such as agents purposefully using goals and data to manage their own operations in ways that ensure task completion meets performance requirements.

Rather than focusing specifically on how data are used, research in public administration has examined the extent to which performance systems have been effective in producing their intended results. Such systems are often adopted in line with agency-theory expectations, suggesting that, if goals were met, performance practices and data would be used purposefully by principals to manage agents. In this light, empirical findings on the effectiveness of the use of performance systems and data are mixed, and positive effects tend to be small in magnitude (Gerrish, 2016).

For instance, in education, the No Child Left Behind Act (NCLB) was found – despite widely documented implementation issues – to be mostly effective. NCLB required the U.S. states to develop performance systems for their schools and, overall, led to improvements in student achievement, including traditionally low-achieving groups (Dee & Jacob, 2011). Lu (2016) examined performance-based contracting within a statewide human services program aimed at helping individuals with disabilities to get employment. He finds that performance contracts improve targeted outcomes, while at the same time have little impact on other important but unmeasured outcomes. Pasha and colleagues (2021), based on a nationwide sample of police departments, show that CompStat performance systems have fairly small effects on targeted crime reduction, but that they significantly increase the risk of arrest for African Americans juveniles, pointing to a major social injustice issue.

In addition to the research on the use and effectiveness of top-down performance systems discussed earlier, other work in public administration examines specific aspects of agency theory related to the use of performance contracts and data. In essence, this research tends to confirm agency theory predictions: more autonomy makes subordinate agencies engage less with central ministries (Bjurstrøm, 2019). Increasing centralization, instead, goes hand in hand with more extensive performance information use (Douglas et al., 2019). Employing performance-driven contracts makes it more likely that agents behave as expected by principals, emphasizing the importance of performance reporting, frequent interactions between principals and agents, and ties between resources allocations and program performance (Han, 2020). The image of the agent matters, too. Nonprofit service providers without profit motives are considered less opportunistic and benefit from more discretion, less monitoring, and longer contracts, although – on average – they do not outperform private providers (Witesman & Fernandez, 2013).

The review of the literature suggests that agency theory plays a central role in scholarship on government performance contracts, systems, and data. This research tends to use the organization as its unit of analysis, which is why the focus is rarely on data use by managers. However, it documents how routines of data reporting and use are formally institutionalized as a part of performance contracts or agreements. For the most part, such performance regimes are considered successful (and data use is deemed purposeful) if agents meet the expectations formally articulated by the principal. While data use within these performance systems can be purposeful, passive, or political, research has also pointed to problems related to perverse and dysfunctional uses, particularly in the presence of consequential rewards and sanctions (Benaine & Kroll, 2020; Bohte & Meier, 2000; Heinrich & Marschke, 2010).

2.3.2 Interactive Dialogue Theory

Moynihan's (2008) interactive dialogue model relaxes some of the assumptions made by agency theory and replaces others. It also challenges some of the beliefs that top-down performance systems tend to be built on; although, such beliefs were not so much postulated in agency theory itself, as they were featured in that theory's applications in public management practice. These beliefs included notions that more data will lead to more control and better decisions, or that a great deal of attention needs to be given to measurement, while questions related to use were neglected. Yet, interactive dialogue theory still models data use via the relationships among actors who behave in line with their self-interests. Moynihan's (2008) original application of the theory was situated in the hierarchical setting of the U.S. government, focusing on the relationships between the central administration and federal agencies.

In a nutshell, the theory argues that performance information use is socially constructed. Since performance information is subjective and ambiguous, different actors may disagree on interpretations of performance as well as which actions to take to improve performance. Institutional values and organizational roles affect the sensemaking of data. Therefore, interactive dialogue routines among several actors are needed to give meaning to performance data and get them used. A dialogue that involves actors representing different interests and organizations is likely to yield divergent interpretations of data, which may be politically used for advocacy. In contrast, a dialogue among a more homogenous group of actors is more likely to result in consensus and may even result in learning or problem solving (for some extensions on dialogue routines, see Jakobsen et al., 2018).

An increasing amount of empirical work has further substantiated some of its assumptions and predictions. Moynihan (2015) uses a set of experiments to show that budget allocations based on performance information are contingent on differences in advocacy, goal ambiguity, and anchoring effects linked to said performance information. Research adopting the politically motivated reasoning framework popularized in the behavioral sciences (Kahan, 2016; see also James et al., 2020) also provides a test of the interactive dialogue theory's claim that varying preexisting beliefs ("biases") will lead to differential interpretations of the same performance information. For example, Baekgaard and colleagues (2019) show that decision-makers are less likely to accurately determine performance if the feedback information provided is not in line with their previous governance preferences. Similarly, interest group advocacy shapes conclusions derived from performance data, but only if the ideology of the decision-maker and the interest group align (Nielsen & Moynihan, 2017).

Interactive dialogue theory is in sync with the idea that performance information use can be institutionalized through the social interactions among actors or organizations. It accepts the notion that performance contracts or agreements formally govern the production of data within the government hierarchy.

However, it also suggests that the way performance information is used is a function of dialogue routines, the composition of the field of actors, and their institutionalized biases. The theory loosely draws on a bounded rationality paradigm and acknowledges the relevance of incentives, although it considers effective incentivization to be based on norms, values, and status rather than high-powered rewards.

2.3.3 Stewardship Theory

Stewardship theory provides an alternative view on the agency problem. While the original context across the two perspectives is the same (a principal needs to delegate a task), in this theory, agents are considered to be stewards with different assumptions about their interests and behaviors. Most broadly, stewards are expected to act in the interest of the principal, and there are at least three reasons why this might be the case (Davis et al., 1997; Schillemans & Bjurstrøm, 2019; Van Slyke, 2007). First, principals tend to pick stewards with aligned interest and goals. Often, in the public sector, services are delivered by providers that do not prioritize profits. Second, stewards may realize that long-term benefits may outweigh short-term rent seeking. That is, providing quality services that meet the principal's expectations will likely increase stability and influence, and it may decrease transaction costs. Third, and in line with self-determination theory (Gagné & Deci, 2005), stewards may get enjoyment and fulfillment out of the provision of quality services, particularly if this is tied to autonomy, unique expertise, and purpose.

The implementation of stewardship approaches requires principals to take risks because they give up control mechanisms prominently featured in agency theory. This may be feasible through the development of trust over time. In her study of lasting organizational partnerships, Getha-Taylor (2019) points out three ways to develop such trust: ensure that communication avoids misunderstandings; train and mentor people on how to collaborate effectively; and become "the kind of partner you want others to be" (p. 42). After all, stewardship-based approaches are likely to be effective in uncertain environments in which flexibility and creativity is required on the part of the steward, and it is difficult to specify all eventualities and contingencies in contracts (Davis et al., 1997).

In its most extreme application, stewardship theory would not require the use of performance data. If goals are aligned, there is no agency problem and no need to engage in performance monitoring. However, as argued before, top-down monitoring is only one out of many functions for using performance information, and we can think of many other purposeful uses of data, without linking them to rewards and sanctions. This may include bottom-up uses, where the steward identifies measures that are helpful for running their operations, or the use of collaborative data reviews.

Empirical research in the area of public administration supports some of the claims made by stewardship theory. Often, due to increasing trust and reputation, relationships evolve over time from principal–agent to principal-steward, with measurement systems becoming less rigid (Poocharoen & Wong, 2016; Van Slyke, 2007). Specifically, performance data tend to be used less for monitoring purposes as relationship length and negotiation ease increase (Henderson & Bromberg, 2015). As mutual trust between partners grows, bottom-up performance practices become more impactful (Bjurstrøm, 2020). At the same time, trust has not always been found to be correlated with the use of contract sanctions (Girth, 2014) or choices to execute less formal control (Krause & Swiatczak, 2021). Relational approaches have been shown to be associated with better service outcomes (Amirkhanyan et al., 2012), although we also know that such stewardship-based methods are more likely to be used when the stakes are low (Askim et al., 2019).

Stewardship theory applications in public administration can involve performance information. However, unlike in agency theory, performance data are not simply used for the purposes of monitoring and incentivization. Use will likely be linked to some of the "softer" purposes listed by Behn (2003), including to motivate, promote, celebrate, learn, and improve. At the same time, data use can be directed bottom up with the steward in the driving seat, employing measures and data for their own management needs as opposed to be complying with external requirements. Use can be institutionalized but this is likely via informal norms or routines as opposed to formal performance agreements or contracts.

2.4 Institutionalized versus Discretionary Use

The three theories discussed above identify important determinants of institutionalized data use. They point to the mechanisms that are built around ideas that can be – although largely simplified – summarized as achieving the following: creating incentives, creating dialogue routines, and creating goal alignment. In that sense, they help us understand how data use can be formally or informally institutionalized via configuring relationships and interactions among actors or organizations.

However, as argued before, some data use behaviors remain discretionary. In fact, a large body of empirical work examines discretionary use, which – in that literature – is referred to as purposeful performance information use. Such behavior has been defined as "largely an individual cognitive process, it cannot be directly observed and, therefore, cannot be directly enforced or rewarded" (Moynihan et al., 2012, p. 469). Since discretionary use is substantially different from institutionalized use, this subsection explores the extent to which agency, interactive dialogue, and stewardship theories can also help explain the former type of use.

We can see some general differences between the literatures on institutionalized and discretionary use, as the latter rarely relies on agency or stewardship theories. This may be because scholarship on discretionary use is not really concerned with the effect of performance systems and the formal or informal configuration of the relationship between actors who report or use performance information. Rather, a core assumption in this literature is that the impact of performance bargains and agreements is limited and, while it is important to account for differences in performance systems, the relevant drivers behind discretionary use are often external to the measurement system (Kroll, 2015a; Moynihan & Pandey, 2010).

Another difference is that that the reference point for discretionary use is the individual (i.e., the manager or decision-maker) and not the organization or dyadic relationship between actors. Furthermore, it is interesting that, although the interactive dialogue model is invoked more often than agency or stewardship theory in the literature on discretionary use, the utilization of performance information is rarely modeled as suggested by that theory as a social interaction where meaning is constructed through dialogue. Thus far, surveys have attempted to capture behavioral self-assessments, while experiments have observed how individuals respond to a manipulated piece of information. Rarely do we see references to group behavior or experimental work that would involve multiple subjects in the same decision-making process.

At the same time, we find similarities across the literatures as well. Elements of the interactive dialogue theory have been examined in relation to discretionary use. As previously mentioned, research on political or institutional biases (often due to motivated reasoning) and its impact on data use takes one core assumption of the interactive dialogue model and tests it with regard to discretionary use behavior. This includes work by Christensen and colleagues (2018) that shows that decision-makers, when engaging in performance practices, tend to reprioritize performance goals based on their governance preferences.

Other work examines some of the theory's predictions about dialogue routines. While performance information use is constructed here as individual (and not group) behavior, research shows how the involvement in dialogue and data review routines, which tend to be social processes, affect managers' self-reports of use. For example, we know that routines fostering discourse and proactive goal prioritization increase discretionary use, although the politicization of such processes can have harmful effects (Kroll & Moynihan, 2021). Further, combinations of routines that tie regular performance tracking to the causal knowledge produced in program evaluations can make performance information more useful (Kroll & Moynihan, 2018).

Overall, we find distinct differences across the two literatures but also some overlap, specifically regarding the use of interactive dialogue theory. However, most of the research on discretionary use seems to be based on alternative theoretical models. I will provide an overview of this work in the subsequent subsection.

2.5 Determinants of Discretionary Use

One stream of the literature is concerned with the effect of different forms of presentation and visualization of performance data on discretionary use. While this research focuses on aspects of the performance system (specifically data reporting), it is very different from an institutional perspective that, for example, agency theory would provide. The latter would be concerned with the selection of measures, reporting standards such as format and timeframe, as well as definitions of rewards and sanctions – all features that could be formalized in a contract. The research on data presentation is different, in that its sheds light on system elements that often remain unspecified even in formal performance regimes. Hence, discretionary use is explained via discretionary choices that managers have to make when operating measurement systems. Such choices include selecting among numbers and graphs, benchmarks, measurement units and ratios, and data sources (James et al., 2020).

Findings from this line of research suggest that the same performance data may lead to different decisions when framed positively as opposed to negatively (as a metaphorical glass half full versus half empty; Belardinelli et al., 2018). While negatively framed performance information generally tends to get more attention, we can say more specifically that managers prioritize goals to improve low-performing areas as opposed to further cultivating high-performing ones (Holm, 2018). With regard to the role of anchoring effects, research suggests that the selection among various benchmarks (George et al., 2020) and references points, such as past performance and targets (Holm, 2017), affect data interpretations. Further, social comparisons tend to be more influential than historical ones (Webeck & Nicholson-Crotty, 2020).

The second stream of the literature suggests that, despite being surrounded by powerful institutions, the data users themselves matter in explaining discretionary use. In addition to managers' "will and skill" (Kroll, 2014) regarding working with data, their authority (role within the hierarchy) affects how managers perceive performance data and use them (Micheli & Pavlov, 2020). Personal values are of relevance as well. We know that managers with a great deal of prosocial motivation are more likely to engage in use because such behavior can be disruptive and require extra effort (Moynihan et al., 2012), and this effect is reinforced if guided by transformational leaders (Kroll & Vogel, 2014).

Data users who embrace a managerial identity are more likely to use performance data but also experience less conflict between managerial and professional values, which then facilitates use as well (Pfiffner, 2019). The role of peers matters, too. Peers who use data make managers also want to engage in such a behavior, but peer pressure also directly fosters use, even if not mediated through shaping intentions (Kroll, 2015b). Along similar lines, managers can serve as intermediaries, where their data use affects the use on the part of employees in different organizational echelons. For example, managers' data use fosters purposeful learning at the frontline if managers engage in problem-solving rather than utilizing data for reward and control (Moynihan et al., 2020). This finding is essential, considering that frontline workers have a general tendency to be skeptical of performance information when it is provided in a top-down manner, as opposed to by colleagues and peers (Petersen, 2020).

The third stream of the literature points to the importance of organizational and context factors (for a more extensive review, see Kroll 2015a). In addition to technical capacity and the sophistication of the performance system, three factors stand out. First, leadership commitment regarding performance practices fosters use because it signals to managers that goals, measures, and data are a priority, and that they are "here to stay" (Dull, 2009; Yang & Hsieh, 2007). Second, stakeholder involvement can have a similar positive effect since interested external stakeholders can help pick the most useful measures but also create urgency and support for evidence-based decision-making (Ho, 2006; Moynihan & Hawes, 2012). Third, an innovative culture facilitates data use due to is focus on learning-based improvements that often requires some type of performance feedback (Folz et al., 2009; Moynihan & Pandey, 2010).

2.6 Collective Use

The purpose of this section is to review some of the research on the two more established types of use, institutionalized and discretionary data use, to see which findings can be adapted to the case of collective use. Collective use remains largely discretionary. Most collaborations tend to share an element of voluntariness, and in the absence of formal lines of authority, it is difficult to mandate data use routines. Among the literatures that contribute to explaining discretionary use, the stream that deals with forms of data presentation has relevance for collaborative use as well (James et al., 2020). One amendment, however, may be that, in collaborative settings, it is likely the same group of people that engages in all different stages of the performance management cycle: collecting, presenting, and using data. What this suggests is that user preferences are already built in decisions regarding data presentation, which makes this variable less exogenous and a little less interesting.

Since collective use draws on the group as the reference point, findings regarding the individual level of the manager seem to be less transferable (Kroll, 2014). However, some of this research did focus on the role of differing managerial and professional identities, which could be relevant, particularly if there is a good amount of variation among group members (Moynihan et al., 2020; Petersen, 2020). Research on context factors has pointed to the importance of stakeholder involvement and organizational culture (Kroll, 2015a). Such stakeholder involvement has a slightly different meaning for collaborations, where relevant stakeholders are supposed to become members of a collaborative's core team as opposed to being solely informed or consulted as they would in a traditional bureaucratic setting.

Culture is likely to be a crucial factor, but I see at least two important deviations from previous research here. One is that it is not clear whether an innovate culture would facilitate data use in a collaborative setting as opposed to a strong group/clan culture. Another is that, in many collaborations that are newly established, culture is a much more endogenous factor than in most public organizations where a culture has grown over a long period of time. If culture becomes a more "controllable" variable, it will also turn into an even more promising determinant of decision-making behavior, such as the use of shared measures.

Among the theories that institutionalized use builds on, the principal–agent approach seems to be the least adaptable from a collaboration perspective (Eisenhardt, 1989; Van Slyke, 2007). Since central assumptions about hierarchical relationships, contracts, and incentives may be difficult to convert to a more horizontal and informal setting, agency theory is unlikely to help explain the foundations of collective data use. Nevertheless, performance practices created around shared measures do follow similar principals as more traditional performance systems, and the latter were at least partially inspired by agency theory.

Even if goals are not set top-down and data not reported bottom-up, some of the classic features of performance systems remain the same. Measures should be strategically linked to priority goals, and they need to be broad enough to track which initiatives and actions prove to be effective. While measures can be linked to higher- and lower-level goals, collaborations need to define a selection of quantifiable key performance indicators. Measures need to capture both controllable outputs (what the groups do) and less controllable outcomes (the groups' societal impact; Kroll, 2021). Along these lines, much of the classic performance management theory can be adapted to shared measures regarding the content of the metrics (Ammons, 2020; Hatry, 2006), while the process of creating and using these measures is likely more collaborative and, hence, different.

Interactive dialogue theory seems to be able to contribute a great deal to our understanding of collective use (Moynihan, 2008). While it generally highlights the importance of group composition, it seems to provide support for two alternative predictions. On one hand, the theory suggests that more diverse groups are more likely to see conflict, due to opposing values, roles, and experiences, which then constrains purposeful data use. Since collaboratives tend to be fairly diverse in terms of group composition, according to this perspective, collective use would likely be diminished. On the other hand, collaborations are likely to become less politicized and contentious than coordination processes within the traditional politico-administrative system, as they are driven by a joint (often single-issue) purpose that may trump individual interests and biases. Based on this view, purposeful data use should become more likely in collaborative settings.

A second contribution of this theory is its emphasis on intentionally structuring the dialogue among group members (Moynihan, 2008). Specifically, it suggests that data will more likely be used purposefully if the dialogue is centered around the idea of organizational learning. To that end, communication processes need to be nonconfrontational and focused on collegial, two-way interactions among equal participants. This description seems to naturally align with the collaborative method. Dialogue structures that meet these requirements are likely to fall into the category of learning forums and are different from classic PerformanceStat meetings, both of which I discussed at an earlier point. Dialogue theory also points to the importance of acknowledging and accounting for participants' institutional biases. As argued by James and colleagues (2020), such biases are more likely to be kept in check or "averaged out" in group settings, which – again – is a finding with immediate relevance for collaborations.

Among the institutional theories, the stewardship approach appears to be very instructive for our understanding of collective data use (Davis et al., 1997; Van Slyke, 2007). While (at least formally) collaboratives have fewer principals, they are made up of a group of stewards. In line with that theory, the goals of these stewards are aligned to the point that all group members tend to care enough about the purpose of the collaborative to voluntarily participate in the joint effort. This is notwithstanding the fact that group members may also have varying organizational interests or be prone to institutional biases. Cumulatively then, the stewardship and dialogue theories seem to offer critical insights into the foundation of collective data use. It is particularly interesting that the stewardship perspective, which has almost played no role in explaining discretionary use, can serve as the backbone of a collective-use model.

The contributions of stewardship theory seem essential and straightforward. In settings such as collaborations, in which formal structures and routines are rarely adequate, the theory emphasizes the role of informal factors. Not all use is discretionary, but some of it can be institutionalized through social norms and shared values. Moreover, whether the collaborative engages in the use of shared measures and data might be a function of several determinants. These include the group's diversity, the social interactions and trust among participants, the way various members engage in leading the collaborative, or the group's shared values. Factors such as the ones listed here can be endogenous to the behavior of (influential) group members, but they are unlikely to be "designed" to the extent to which we have control over formalized systems, contracts, or regulations. The next section will further elucidate factors that can impact collective data use but have received little attention in conventional, organizational performance management theory.

3 Explaining the Collective Use of Performance Data

Relational approaches in the realm of stewardship theory have been employed in research on performance agreements among organizations but are rarely adopted in performance information use research, which conceptualizes such behavior as discretionary and located at the level of the individual. As argued previously, research on collective use could benefit from adopting a relational perspective to explain how collective behavior varies along with different group dynamics and configurations. In this section, I refer to performance data use more generally, although at times, I speak of shared measures when differences between the two concepts are of theoretical relevance.

I theorize the role of six relational factors that may help explain collective data use. First, while group diversity can increase conflict regarding the interpretation of data, it may also help balance discussions and generate fresh ideas needed to link data to action. Second, egalitarian decision-making structures can ensure that a vast majority of group members can share in the discussion of performance information, thereby, expanding the knowledge base and the group's expertise. Third, high-quality social relationships facilitate the sharing of performance data and the building of trust, which reduces transaction costs of the decision-making process. Fourth, distributed leadership increases the group's ownership of the collaborative endeavor and members' interest in group achievements as well as related measures and evidence. Fifth, a strong group (clan) culture may create a safe and supportive environment in which members are motivated to experiment with data-based learning. Finally, sixth, value congruence makes it more likely that shared goals and measures will be considered legitimate, ensuring that performance data receive more attention, while also providing a joint cognitive frame to foster sensemaking processes.

3.1 Group Composition

One factor that is often associated with group composition is the group's diversity. Groups can be demographically (in terms of gender, race, ethnicity, and age) and functionally (in terms of varying educational, professional, organizational backgrounds, and expertise) diverse (Horwitz & Horwitz, 2007; Moon & Christensen, 2020). Most broadly, diversity has been associated with positive work outcomes, which is part of the appeal behind bringing together a range of different actors for the purpose of a collaboration. A second compositional factor is the adequateness of the group makeup. Adequateness may overlap with diversity to the extent that legitimacy-based adequateness (or representativeness) can likely be achieved by involving all relevant stakeholders, which also facilitates diversity. At the same time, a group can consist of a good mix of actors but may not be adequately composed if, for example, a collaboration that addresses a public health issue misses the necessary public health experts. The governance structure can be a crucial success factor because unless a group is perceived to be legitimate in terms of representation, it will be very difficult for the collaboration to move forward.

The "business case" for group diversity is as follows. More diverse teams are likely to produce better results because the variety of expertise, experience, and perspectives that they offer may yield more innovative and creative solutions to a given problem (Duchek et al., 2020; Moon & Christensen, 2020). Even if heterogeneity among members leads to conflict, such conflict can still be productive and lead to better decisions or outcomes (King et al., 2009).

However, additional research has contributed to further qualifying the positive diversity effect, drawing a picture that looks more balanced overall. Pelled and colleagues (1999) showed that effects vary across types of diversity and conflict. Functional diversity leads to task conflict, which is more the productive type, while demographic diversity fosters less constructive emotional conflict.

Similarly, Moon and Christensen (2020) theorize that functional diversity is more effective than demographic diversity, although their empirical findings are mixed and moderated by organizational climate. Data from U.S. marine aquaculture collaborations suggest that relational learning among members is facilitated by diversity in beliefs, not organizational affiliations, although both are on the functional side of diversity (Siddiki et al., 2017). Further, moderate levels of diversity, which means a balance between diversity and unity, can be more effective in fostering fair decision-making processes among collaboration members (Kim & Siddiki, 2018).

In line with the literature summarized earlier, expectations for the effect of group diversity on performance information use may be similarly mixed. On one hand, diversity can harm purposeful data use if differences in opinion and interpretations become adversarial and contentious (Moynihan, 2008) – although diversity in such settings refers to variation in values, roles, and experiences, not demographics. Such a view follows a where-I-stand-depends-on-where-I-sit paradigm: members representing very different interests and organizations are less likely to agree on a shared pattern of sensemaking of data, let alone agree on consequential actions informed by the data. Specifically, the more "political" the setting – that is, the more public, high-stake, and "zero-sum" – the less likely it is that group diversity will yield the purposeful use of performance data.

On the other hand, the diversity and adequateness of a group's composition may foster purposeful use. A group whose makeup is considered to be adequate to address the problem at hand is more likely to possess the right expertise needed to understand relevant data and the causal links behind various actions and their impact. Similarly, both demographic and functional diversity can help generate a variety of ideas needed to improve shared measures and data use. Finding useful measures requires controversial discussions of the validity, reliability, and feasibility of potential metrics and data sources, and developing strategies to counteract negative performance trends often needs out-of-the-box thinking (Kroll, 2015a; Moynihan & Hawes, 2012).

Research has shown that performance data receive more attention in the presence of functional diversity because using goals, measures, and data is one avenue to systematically leverage the potential diversity benefits (especially in otherwise stagnant environments; Andersen & Moynihan, 2016). Further, diverse groups have been found to get more out of their knowledge sharing with actors outside of the group because group diversity makes it more likely to obtain new information from different sources that adds to, rather than replicates, existing internal knowledge (Cummings, 2004). Finally, diversity can help keep individual biases in check and challenge bad decisions that can be the result of groupthink (Janis, 1991). It may help to prevent sensemaking of performance information driven by group loyalty and the suppression of dissenting views at the expense of critical thinking.

3.2 Egalitarian Structure

The structure of collaborations, which consist of members from multiple organizations, tends to be "flatter" than that of the traditional organization, especially those of agencies within the Weberian bureaucracy (Bryson et al., 2015; Emerson & Nabatchi, 2015a; Isett et al., 2011). While formal hierarchies and authority resulting from the positioning within an organization-like structure are largely absent, collaborations – also conceptualized as "heterarchies" (Kontopoulos, 1993, p. 55ff.) – are not necessarily a horizontal conglomerate of equal actors. Some collaborations are led by one of the member organizations or participants create a new "network administrative organization" for the purpose of managing the group (Provan & Kenis, 2008). But even within these governance arrangements, some collaborations may be more centralized than others. One way to get a better sense as to how egalitarian a collaborative tends to be is by examining formal and informal decision-making structures and routines.

Decision-making practices can fall on a spectrum with centralized attributes on one side (routines that are "top-down" or discussions that are "dominated by a few") versus a strong consensus orientation and the active involvement of most members on the other side. One reason behind opting for collaborative governance often is the realization that a vertically centralized, regulative approach may not be sufficiently effective. But to truly leverage the benefits that collaboration can offer, decision-making needs to be open to broad input and participation. In fact, a natural experiment shows that collaborations, if managed well, can produce a creative advantage over more traditional bureaucratic settings in that the choices made across governance regimes only overlapped by about 50 percent (Doberstein, 2016). A study of 307 coded published cases of public environmental decision-making found that environmental standards were significantly improved if the decision-making was participatory; this was operationalized via high communication intensity and the delegation of power (Jager et al., 2020).

Along these lines, management research has emphasized the value of participatory decision-making in organizations. A meta-analysis finds that employee participation fosters job satisfaction, commitment, involvement, and motivation (Spector, 1986), although some participative mechanisms have been found to be more effective than others (Cotton et al., 1988). For example, participation in phases of the decision cycle, such as planning and generating alternatives, tends to be most impactful (Black & Gregersen, 1997). To be consequential, at times, participation needs to be paired with additional variables such as managerial competence as a study of the school system shows (Grissom, 2012).

Research on collaborations and activist groups tends to discuss participation through the lens of inclusiveness. Johnston and colleagues (2011) emphasize two conditions of successful inclusion: setting aside extra time to be able to reach a consensus, and onboarding of new members through initial contact with only a subset of the collaborative's members. Additional such factors include the use of subgroups and an initial focus on tasks that are "low-hanging fruits" (Doberstein, 2016) as well as assigning responsibility to all members for monitoring domineering behaviors, reflecting as a group on the distribution of power, and treating decisions as largely provisional (Leach, 2016).

Drawing on the research cited earlier, I expect that egalitarian decision-making structures, based on consensus and participation, will likely increase performance information use. There is evidence for a collaborative advantage when it comes to data use. Here, a diverse set of stakeholders can help select the "right" measures, obtain and integrate data from different organizations, and make collective sense of what the data suggest. However, to leverage such benefits, collaborations need to actively engage all members. Research has shown that decision-makers embedded in intensively networked environments are more likely to use performance information (Moynihan & Hawes, 2012). Further, egalitarian environments have been associated with an effective dialogue about performance and performance data (Van Dooren et al., 2015, p. 165). In the absence of power struggles and the use (and abuse) of authority, the politicization of data may become less likely, and information use may instead become more purposeful.

3.3 Social Relationships

Research on social capital emphasizes the importance of frequent interactions and trusting relationships within collectives (Leana & Van Buren, 1999; Nahapiet & Ghoshal, 1998). Similarly, work on team-member exchange makes the case for the critical role of the quality of relationships and reciprocal exchanges among peers within work groups (Banks et al., 2014; Seers, 1989). Both literatures find support for the effect of high-quality relationships on information and knowledge sharing (Chen, 2018; Lee et al., 2015). Specifically, social capital is said to facilitate the combination and exchange of intellectual capital, which may lead to the creation of new knowledge (Nahapiet & Ghoshal, 1998). In addition to fostering knowledge sharing, high-quality, trusting relationships can help develop shared mental models (Willems, 2016) and reduce conflict and, hence, the need for bargaining and formal monitoring, which leaves more room for creativity and the development of new ideas and approaches (Liu, 2013).

My general expectation is that social capital will foster the purposeful use of performance information. That is, groups whose members work well together, share information, establish patterns of communication, and develop relational trust are more likely to consider performance data in their decision-making. However, it is worth noting that, while social capital has been found to facilitate the sharing of information generally, it is possible that groups with a great deal of social capital prefer using information other than performance data (Tantardini & Kroll, 2015). On one hand, groups characterized by high-quality relationships may opt for information from informal, nonroutine sources – such as conversations, stories, or observations – as opposed to data produced via formal performance systems. On the other hand, social capital could be much better aligned with shared measures compared to other performance data, since the latter often originate from group-external accountability systems. Instead, shared measures intrinsically reflect some of the group's social capital as they were jointly agreed upon, span across multiple organizations, and tap into improvements that are considered the group's shared responsibility.

While empirical evidence is still scarce, initial findings suggest that public organizations with more social capital have a preference for both using nonroutine as well as routine performance feedback (Tantardini, 2019). It seems fairly plausible that information flow, established via a dense and interactive network structure, will benefit data use. One consideration is that performance practices in collaborations – owing to the involvement of multiple independent organizations – are even more siloed than those across departments within the same organization. Hence, a reliable structure of binding ties may add even more value for collaboratives, helping to ensure that many stakeholders are aware, and have access to, all relevant performance data, and that different data from various organizations can be integrated (Tantardini & Kroll, 2015). Similarly, scholarship has emphasized the importance of dialogue and review routines to facilitate data use (Moynihan & Kroll, 2016), which reiterates the utility of structural social capital for collaborations.

Another relevant relational factor is the creation of trust among group members. Trust refers to one person's belief that another person's intended actions will be appropriate (Nahapiet & Ghoshal, 1998). Social capital is based on resilient trust that is not unique to single interactions but relates to beliefs about a person's moral integrity (Leana & Van Buren, 1999). Trust may facilitate the use of performance data in at least three ways. First, it will help group members to see data-informed decision-making as a good-faith effort for the purpose of real improvements as opposed to more political types of use associated with maximizing individual interests or personal gain. Second, trust can also reduce transaction costs when working with performance data, as it increases one's confidence in group members' data and their interpretation thereof. Finally, a crucial function of trust is to make group members feel comfortable sharing information about bad performance or failure, which can be important puzzle pieces for improvement strategies but are far too often hidden or willingly misconstrued.

3.4 Distributed Leadership

Distributed leadership is "conceived of as a collective social process emerging through the interactions of multiple actors" (Bolden, 2011, p. 251; see also Ospina, 2016). Distributed leadership, which is often also referred to as shared or collective leadership, directs attention away from formally appointed individuals and instead promotes the idea that leadership roles are dispersed across group members. In that sense, leadership is an emergent group phenomenon characterized by the ways peers influence each other laterally (Zhu et al., 2018). Distributed leadership is different from participation as explained in subsection 3.2. The participation literature is about the inclusion of group members in the making of decisions for the purpose of consensus building, whereas distributed leadership expects members to take the lead on actively managing the group and its processes.

Group members may share in leadership functions such as planning and organizing, problem solving, support and consideration, or development and mentoring (Hiller et al., 2006). Leadership can be distributed in ways in which group members engage together in specific roles and behaviors, members take turns over time, or different members take the lead on different activities or perform different functions (Zhu et al., 2018). Meta-analyses show that distributed or shared leadership is positively related to team-level work outcomes. Effects seem to be stronger for attitudinal outcomes and behavioral processes relative to team performance, and they are moderated by levels of task interdependence (Wang et al., 2014; Wu et al., 2020).

One mechanism through which distributed leadership can facilitate performance information use is creating ownership of performance improvements and, by extension, measures and data. Distributed leadership moves members from being just one among many stakeholders to members who are actively involved in the management and coordination of the group. As members' engagement increases, their stakes rise too, and they are likely to feel more ownership of the group's success and performance. Caring about performance, in turn, is related to an interest in discussing goals and measures as well as using data to track and improve performance (Ammons & Rivenbark, 2008). Using language from social identity theory, distributed leadership is likely to yield the formation of a larger in-group and a smaller out-group within a collaborative (Tajfel & Turner, 2004). Along these lines, groups with a higher level of distributed leadership can create a collective sense of ownership of the collaborative effort, and the latter has been found to foster performance data use (Kroll, 2014).

While a fair amount of scholarship, such as the meta-analyses cited earlier, are concerned with the effect of distributed leadership on work outcomes, some research shows that this leadership approach leads to more functional organizing and planning processes (Choi et al., 2017). Similarly, work on distributed leadership interventions in schools demonstrates real changes in the processes in which schools were managed (Supovitz & Tognatta, 2013). Though more research is certainly needed, it seems that distributed leadership helps creating collective capacity that is needed to manage groups more effectively, which is also a known prerequisite for successfully using formal data-driven approaches.

Another mechanism is built around the notion of creativity. Distributed leadership has been found to foster creativity through knowledge sharing and creative self-efficacy. Creative solutions to problems require the exchange and discussion of new ideas, which is likely to occur when a majority of group members is actively engaged in the leadership of dynamic group processes (Gu et al., 2018). At the same time, distributed leadership through its focus on the sharing of influence and its openness toward bottom-up processes will increase members' self-efficacy to participate in creative endeavors (He et al., 2020). Creativity is an important factor in performance data use, particularly since it is often far from clear which actions to take in the presence of good or bad performance. New ideas are needed to reengineer processes or reimagine implementing a program for the purpose of widening reach and strengthening impact.

3.5 Group Culture

Organizational culture is broadly understood as the shared informal norms, values, and beliefs that shape behavior, which can be related to, but are distinguishable from, formal structures and processes. Culture has been described as "how we do things," rituals serving as glue for the purpose of integration, idiosyncratic symbols and language, the social control system, or the organization's immune system (Watkins, 2013). Schein (1990) argues that culture manifests itself at three levels: artifacts, values, and underlying assumptions. Artifacts, including symbols, stories, and myths, are easy to observe, although they can also be misleading to the external observer when observed by themselves. The next level are the espoused and documented values, norms, ideologies, charters, and philosophies. Most hidden values include an organization's taken-for-granted and often unconscious assumptions that shape members' perceptions and thought processes. The iceberg metaphor of culture suggests that only the smallest part is visible, whereas the bigger part is more difficult to see and understand.

In terms of culture content, that is, typologies that explain the extent to which cultures may differ, Douglas's (1996) group-grid matrix popularized by Hood (2000) has been prominently featured in the public administration literature, as depicted in Figure 4(a). In essence, the typology proposes four types of culture based on the combinations of the role of rules (grid) and a focus on the collective versus individual (group). A "hierarchist" culture emphasizes forms of established authority and the importance of rules for governing the collective. A "sectarian–egalitarian" culture focuses on lateral group processes and rejects social distinction. An "individualist" culture is associated with taking chances and risks as well as competition among individuals. A "fatalist" culture emphasizes social isolation, skepticism, fate, and the ritualistic following of rules without gaining group loyalty (Hood, 2012; Van Dooren et al., 2015).

Another widely used typology in the public administration literature is the competing values framework (e.g., Calciolari et al., 2018; Moynihan & Pandey, 2007). The framework was developed by Cameron and Quinn (2011), who proposed a two-by-two culture matrix mapped along a control-flexibility and an internal-external orientation axis, as shown in Figure 4(b). A bureaucratic

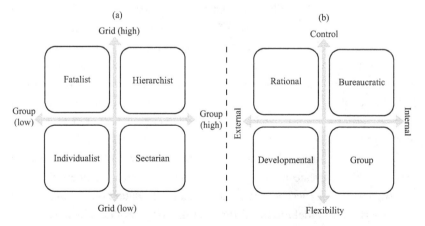

Figure 4 Culture typologies: (a) group-grid and (b) competing values

culture's focus is on control, doing things right, and incrementalism. It is concerned with planning, efficient processes, and enforcing compliance, while emphasizing predictability and minimizing errors. A group culture is characterized by collaboration, doing things together, and long-term development. It is known for unified behaviors, cohesion, and commitment to the community, and it has also been described as a clan culture. A developmental culture, in turn, is about creativity, doing things first, and innovation. It highlights values such as experimentation, flexibility, and adaptability, and it tends to have a strong change orientation. Further, a rational culture focuses on competing, doing things fast, and short-term performance. It emphasizes the market, speed, and getting results.

Both typologies shown in Figure 4 share some commonalities (compare the right-hand sides of each matrix), mostly because both highlight the importance of grid or control, respectively, and use a focus on the group or the internal as a central dimension. Both typologies may also support similar expectations for the use of performance data within collaborations. Hood (2012) argues varying cultures have different preferences for the use of performance management practices. Hierarchist cultures lean toward top-down target systems, and individualist cultures lean toward competition via performance rankings. Sectarian–egalitarian cultures, the category that most collaborations would fall in, are likely to use data as intelligence, that is, to inform decisions, a practice that mirrors the idea of data-informed decision-making.

The competing values framework may similarly suggest that a strong group culture can be linked to data-driven decisions in collaborations. Interestingly, with respect to government agencies, research has shown that those with developmental cultures tend to engage more in performance information use (e.g., Kroll, 2015a; Moynihan & Pandey, 2010). Here, it seems that data are used to explore the effectiveness of new ways of doings things, and that performance practices can be well aligned with a change orientation. This might be different for collaborations. In collaborative settings, it is more difficult to identify, and agree upon, formal goals and measures of progress. Further, collaborations themselves are often an organizational innovation, with less history, stability, and attached bureaucracy than the typical government agency, which makes organizational change and development less relevant driving forces. Instead, collaborations may likely utilize data if they are able to create a strong group culture in which members feel safe and supported to experiment with, and engage in, data-based learning, and where performance definitions also reflect the long-term development of the group.

3.6 Value Congruence

The term value congruence refers to members of a group sharing the same normative beliefs about what is desirable (Edwards & Cable, 2009). It can also be understood as a value-based type of person-group fit (Kristof-Brown et al., 2005). Value congruence has been found to be positively associated with work group effectiveness (Hoffman et al., 2011), partially through the creation of a strong team identity (Mitchell et al., 2012). While such cognitive alignment often naturally grows as the result of social processes, research has demonstrated that said processes can be managed via the use of more formal systems (Paarlberg & Perry, 2007). In addition to performance effects, a strong person-group fit fosters crucial workplace attitudes such as job satisfaction, organizational commitment, or the intention to stay (Kristof-Brown et al., 2005). A mechanism that links value congruence to positive work attitudes is via increasing buy-in into the organization's vision and, hence, connecting individuals to the workplace (Ryu, 2015).

One way in which value congruence can foster performance data use is through improving communication routines and the predictability of behaviors and decision outcomes in groups (Edwards & Cable, 2009). It facilitates creating a common cognitive frame for the sensemaking of events, which can benefit the sharing and interpretation of performance information. This means that, if groups, despite individuals' different backgrounds and experiences, develop values and language that are shared across members, discussions about performance data may become more productive and decision-making more consensual. Work groups have been found to be powerful prisms through which individuals experience the entire organization (Kroll et al., 2019), and mental models shared among members tend to be important predictors of group behaviors and actions (Mohammed et al., 2010).

Shared values and purposes are two related but distinguishable concepts. A shared purpose often brings individuals from different organizations together and makes them join a collaboration effort. However, individuals can work toward a joint purpose while still maintaining separate interests, priorities, and values. Only the development of congruent values will likely reduce political uses of performance data and foster purposeful use. Value congruence makes it more likely for members to act in the group's joint interest as opposed to their separate individual interest, because in such a scenario, dominant individual and group values as well as priorities have been aligned. This reduces the probability that members use performance data to advocate for actions or decisions that would only benefit single organizations.

If values, goals, and priorities are largely shared, we would generally expect less conflict around performance data, and the latter will be seen as a legitimate source of feedback to track progress toward common objectives. But more acceptance of the same interpretation of data can also be counterproductive. Research shows that value congruence can lead to both more cooperative voice as well as silence, depending on other context factors (Wang et al., 2012). On one hand, it is possible that shared values will facilitate information sharing, whereas on the other hand, it may suppress dissenting views and interpretations of data. All in all, however, performance information will likely receive more attention in decision-making if the objectives they capture and the values behind them are widely shared (Tantardini & Kroll, 2015).

4 Case Study: Opioid-Response Collaborations in North Carolina

This section examines the extent to which the theoretical ideas put forward in the previous section contribute to better understanding the collaborative use of shared measures. It employs a case study of community collaboratives in North Carolina that were established to address the prevalent opioid epidemic. Blending qualitative and quantitative evidence, this section describes the collaborative work with shared measures and explains differences in data use behavior among community groups.

4.1 Background

Opioids are substances used for pain relief, including prescription opioids – such as methadone, oxycodone (e.g., OxyContin), and hydrocodone (e.g., Vicodin) – as well as heroin and fentanyl (a synthetic opioid; CDC, 2021a). The term "opioid epidemic" refers to the overuse of prescription and illicit painkillers that has led to addiction and death, creating a public health crisis with detrimental effects on entire communities across the United States. It was declared a national public health emergency in 2017. While there have always been problems around illegal opioid use, the recent epidemic has been fueled by three waves of overdose deaths: alarming increases in the use and abuse of prescription opioids starting in the 1990s; a rise in deaths involving heroin beginning in 2010 (for which prescription opioids often served as a gateway drug); and deaths related to illicitly manufactured fentanyl starting in 2013 (CDC, 2021a; Jones et al., 2018; NIDA, 2021).

Between 1999 and 2019, nearly 500,000 people died from an overdose involving prescription and illicit opioids. While the number of opioid prescriptions peaked in 2012 at about 250 million, the number of opioid-related overdose fatalities has steadily increased over the last two decades (CDC, 2021a; b). Overdose deaths seemed to have stagnated between 2017 and 2018 at a high level (NIDA, 2021) but increased again in 2019 and, as preliminary statistics indicate, have reached a record high during the COVID-19 pandemic (Katz & Sanger-Katz, 2021). The most recent year for which complete data are available is 2019. During that year alone, nearly 50,000 people died because of opioid overdoses (NIDA, 2021), and about 9.7 million people misused prescription opioids (HHS, 2021). NIDA (2021) reports that the economic burden of prescription opioid abuse, comprised of costs for care, treatment, and the criminal justice complex, is estimated to be $78.5 billion per year.

The opioid epidemic has been called a "North American phenomenon" (Shipton et al., 2018, p. 23). While the causes behind it are complex, at least three factors tend to stand out in the context of the United States: liberalized rules and the related prescription culture within the medical profession; aggressive – in part illegal – marketing efforts on the part of pharmaceutical companies; and the U.S. health insurance system. In the late 1990s, the professional medical community declared pain assessment and management as one of its main objectives, leading to the increased use of prescription opioids for chronic, noncancer pain. At this point, the culture among medical professionals began to shift from preventing addiction to prioritizing pain relief (Jones et al., 2018; Shipton et al., 2018).

Aggressive and illicit marketing schemes were another factor, as the infamous case of Purdue Pharma and its marketing of OxyContin illustrates. In November 2020, the company pleaded guilty to criminal charges related to its OxyContin sales and agreed to pay penalties of $8.3 billion in a settlement with the U.S. Justice Department. Purdue Pharma defrauded federal health agencies, marketed OxyContin to doctors who were suspected of writing illegal prescriptions, convinced doctors to prescribe OxyContin even when unnecessary, and paid illegal kickbacks (Hoffman & Benner, 2020). In the early 2000s, prescriptions of OxyContin rose from 670,000 to 6.2 million (Jones et al., 2018). Lastly, relative to other countries, health insurance in the United States has been described as a system with a tendency to pay for "cheap" pills rather than expensive therapies, even in cases in which the former is known to have little effect (Amos, 2017).

The opioid epidemic has been characterized as a "wicked problem" (Lee, 2018, p. 51), with no easy solution and multiple intertwined, nonlinear streams of causes and consequences. Specifically, Lee illustrates the complexity of the problem as follows:

> "Those who advocate for reducing opioid prescribing fail to see the Ohio experience where opioid use simply went underground or shifted to illicit

drugs. Those who advocate for no adjustment to opioid prescribing fail to see the correlation between prescribing and overdoses observed in many communities. Those who argue that this is purely a problem of social determinants of health fail to see the overdose and addiction rates in affluent communities. Those who argue that medication assisted treatment (MAT) will solve the problem fail to see that most patients who are prescribed MAT do not continue it, and in fact relapse to opioids. ... Those who push an access-to-care argument fail to see that access is just the first step – we need appropriate utilization of resources. Those who are going after the "opioid crisis" fail to see that over 50% of opioids in the US are prescribed to people with mental health conditions and unless we treat those underlying mental disorders, we cannot solve this problem. (p. 51)"

Calls for integrated approaches that bring together stakeholders with different expertise and resources to address the issue have become more frequent and prominent. Along these lines, Vivek Murthy (2016), then Surgeon General of the United States, concluded that "the opioid epidemic cannot be solved by government alone. It will require the engagement and leadership of all segments of society ... " (p. 2415). The North Carolina case featured a program that promoted the creation of collaboratives at the community level to address the opioid epidemic and provided training and support including on the management of such groups and the use of shared measures (Nelson, 2021; SOG, 2021).

With regard to the crisis context, North Carolina largely mirrored the trends at the national level described earlier (NCDHHS, 2021a). Despite a fair amount of variation, the aggregate opioid mortality rate increased more in nonmetro as opposed to metro areas in the United States over the last two decades (Monnat, 2020). When comparing mortality rates across states based on the numbers from only the nonmetro counties between 2014 and 2016, North Carolina fell in the second highest quartile with rates between 10 and 15 per 100,000 (Monnat, 2020). In 2017, North Carolina's Opioid Action Plan was released and since then has been associated with reductions in opioid dispensing and increases in the use of drugs to treat opioid disorders, particularly treatments for uninsured and Medicaid patients (NCDHHS, 2021b).

To address the epidemic at the community level in North Carolina, the SOG at UNC-Chapel Hill ran a two-year program (the Opioid Response Project) in which support, guidance, and training was provided to the members of ten local opioid-response collaboratives from across the state. The program consisted of webinars, supplemental materials, and forums (i.e., meetings wherein members from the different groups came together and received input and training on topics related to collaboration, team management, and opioid-specific topics). Further, the SOG faculty served as group liaisons who provided insights and feedback to the groups and, on occasion, attended their community meetings.

The program followed a modified collective-impact model that broadly covered areas such as a common agenda, mutually reinforcing activities, continuous communication, and organizational support (Nelson, 2021). Further, one key aspect of the collective impact model and of the work of the ten groups was working with shared performance practices and measures, which is the topic of interest for this Element. The collaboratives consisted of members representing a variety of organizations, including health providers, local governments, health departments, legal courts, law enforcement, emergency medical services, social services, as well as members of the civil society such as physicians, researchers, or parents. Most groups were structured using three organizational layers: a leadership team, work groups (organized by subject matter), and the community group as a whole (the entire task force).

4.2 Use of Shared Measures

Based on interviews and document reviews, I now explore the nature of shared measures in the Opioid Response Project. Shared measures in this case were found in three areas: attached to higher-level goals; found at the operational level within action plans; and they showed up – more inductively but routinely – in group discussions. As the priorities across groups and communities varied, their goals and measures did too. But broadly, shared measures at the highest goal level tended to focus on outputs and outcomes. Examples of this include the number of overdose prevention kits distributed, number of active campaigns, or number of people screened (all outputs) as well as the number of pills dispensed, number of overdose fatalities, or number of repeat calls (all outcomes).

The action plans also included measures attached to specific initiatives that were often used to track the completion of individual steps taken toward the achievement of the long-term goals. Examples of this include measures created around the mapping and identification of services, such as the number of offerings of Hepatitis C treatments for people using drugs or the number of potential treatment providers and emergency departments. Other measures found in the action plans were engagement metrics as well as indicators that range from inputs to (intermediate) outcomes. Such examples include the number of participants in events or meetings, number of trainings and presentations provided, or the number of clicks or interactions on a website.

While shared measures tended to be used intentionally rather than on an ad hoc basis (i.e., data collection was based on predefined measures that were tied to goals), the identification of such measures could be a nonlinear, iterative process. Some groups invited externals speakers and professionals who provided data as part of presentations on specific subjects. In several cases, these data seemed relevant to the group and resulted in the group including them in regular data updates and discussions. This somewhat randomly acquired information could therefore turn into a shared measure. It is noteworthy that the groups were newly formed and did not start out with an established, fully developed set of measures. Hence, it was not uncommon that measures morphed from being interesting but group-external and somewhat random to becoming intentionally integrated into the group's shared measures.

To learn more about the incorporation of shared measures in decision-making, I surveyed members about each group's data use practices based on items adapted from Moynihan and colleagues (2012) (see Table 3). The items were adapted via a referent shift from "I" to "we," so that they capture perceptions of group rather than individual behavior. The first four items capture different aspects of group-internal use, such as setting priorities or identifying problems, while the latter three items tap into the idea of external use for more political or communication-related purposes. However, the results from the factor analysis in Table 3 suggest that all seven items load on a single factor, meaning that use in one area is correlated with use in all others. This is interesting as it deviates from the two-factor structure proposed by Moynihan

Table 3 Factor analysis of shared measures use

Item	Factor loading	Uniqueness
We regularly use performance data to make decisions	0.919	0.155
We use performance data to think of new approaches for doing old things	0.937	0.121
We use performance data to set priorities	0.927	0.140
We use performance data to identify problems that need attention	0.937	0.123
We use performance data to communicate achievements to stakeholders	0.921	0.152
We use performance data to advocate for resources to support our collaborative's needs	0.938	0.121
We use performance data to explain the value of our work to the public	0.856	0.267

Note: Principal component factoring was applied; the factor's Eigenvalue is 5.92 and no additional factors were significant. Items were measured using a seven-point scale. Data: Main Survey (Part 2), n = 136.

and colleagues where internal managerial uses were distinguishable from external political ones. In essence, shared measures use in this case study seemed to be a one-dimensional construct, and differences in use were more likely to be found across groups than across purposes.

Groups that reported frequent data use often devoted segments of their meetings to review data. Such reviews tended to be driven by available data as opposed to an overview of all the relevant metrics. Here, data use had been described as informing decisions rather than determining them, driving conversations around topics, and being sufficiently helpful to plan next steps. Use was often limited due to issues related to baseline data and data integration. In some instances, baseline metrics were still missing, mostly for key measures attached to higher-level goals that were aspirational and reflected future needs. In other cases, baseline metrics were collected but either reference points were missing or the groups had not been able to link the existing data to current discussions or upcoming decisions. With regard to data integration, groups dealt with the challenge that the data were collected by several organizations using different formats or even definitions. Here, simply compiling data reports on a somewhat regular basis required a great deal of time and resources. In one of my interviews, one collaborator summarized how the process of treating patients was highly fragmented, resulting in data collection problems:

> People that come in off the street who present in the emergency department who are then screened and offered MAT [Medication-Assisted Treatment] and a warm hand-off to a treatment provider. Each one of those stops is a different data system. In some cases, there is not even a good connection between the stops.

While high performing groups (such as group A) fit with the general data use pattern described earlier, including the documented limitations, lower performing groups (such as group B) did not (for more information on both groups, see Figure 5). In fact, there was fairly little documentation of shared measures use in group B. If data were discussed, then these were mostly ad hoc metrics rather than shared measures that would link overarching goals and operations. The group seemed stuck at the formalization stage of goals and measures, without having made the leap toward routine data collection and use. So, while collaborative documents had been produced, plans were not fully completed, let alone implemented.

The interviews with the groups and trainers provided some additional insights into the use of shared measures. Some groups developed their own surveys to collect information that was not stored as a part of existing agency

Figure 5 Identification strategy of groups A and B

When documenting and explaining the groups' shared measures use in this and the next subsections, I will draw on observations from all ten groups but contrast two of the groups in particular. I selected the two groups – I refer to them as "A" and "B" – based on stark differences in terms of their development and use of shared measures.

Group A was doing well, whereas group B was struggling.

The purpose behind giving more attention to these two groups is creating reference points for the interpretation of my qualitative data. I think readers will be better able to make sense of my examples, observations, and quotes when being able to link them to the recurring settings of groups A and B.

The selection process was as follows. I conducted a document analysis in which I reviewed and assessed all groups' performance measurement sheets as well as their interconnectedness with the groups' goal and vision documents and action plans. I ranked the performance sheets along the criteria strategic relevance, measurability, and completeness using a five-point scale.

Based on this assessment, group A was among the top three and group B among the bottom three. While my assessment drew on the groups' plans and intentions rather than actions and actual performance, my interviews with the trainers confirmed these choices. When asked about all groups' progress trainers independently mentioned group A as one of the top performers related to measure use and group B consistently among those at the bottom in terms of their development and use of performance data. Once I began collecting more data on both groups, additional evidence supported this notion.

records. Another topic was the place where data use was located. In some cases, the leadership-team members were the most active data users, while in other cases, use occurred in the working groups or even the community-wide task forces. A finding that emphasizes the unique nature of collective data use is that it is likely to be most impactful when focused on goals that span across organizational borders, requiring a diverse set of actors to truly collaborate. One of the trainers spoke to this point:

> I had to push them to . . . not think about just goals that they as a small group [of local government employees] could accomplish on their own. But what can they accomplish if they partner with one of the other members of the collaborative, and what kind of combined goals can you come up with? . . . It really wasn't taking advantage of the collaborative.

4.3 Determinants of Collective Use

To explain differences in the collective use of shared measures, I first turn to the surveys and then incorporate the interviews results. More specifically, I begin with a regression analysis that employs the items listed in Table 3 to construct a factor score for "shared measures use" that serves as the dependent variable. This factor score is regressed on a set of explanatory variables that map onto the concepts featured in Section 3. The purpose here is to examine whether the previously theorized variables contribute to better understanding differences in shared measures use and to identify more and less important determinants.

All explanatory variables are drawn from the Main Survey (Part 2). While I provide an overview of their measures here, a complete list of all survey items, their scales, and reliability scores can be found in the Appendix. The first variable is group composition, which is a two-item construct that captures the diversity of the group ("a wide range of people") as well as the extent to which "the right people" were involved. The second variable is egalitarian structure, which assesses differences in the group's decision-making styles and, thereby, differentiates flat from more hierarchical group structures. Three items tap into this concept that – since they are not highly correlated – are used as separate measures of different subdimensions. Two measures are formulated in reverse, that is, they capture the opposite of an egalitarian structure – "a top-down structure" and "discussions dominated by a few people." The final measure is regarding the existence of a consensus-oriented decision-making style.

The third variable is social relationships. It is a combined scale of four items that quantifies the extent to which group members "work well together," "trust each other," as well as "communicate well" and "share information effectively" with each other. The fourth variable is distributed leadership. It is constructed based on the work by Hiller and colleagues (2006) and uses eight items from their scale out of which four item pairs represent the following dimensions: group members' engagement in the leadership activities of planning and organizing; problem solving; support and consideration; as well as development and mentoring. All items are highly correlated and makeup one index. The fifth and final variable is value congruence. This is a two-item construct that captures the extent to which values are shared among group members as well as the existence of a joint purpose.

Regarding the modeling of relationships, the first choice is that of control variables. I account for perceived differences in available resources, which might affect both group dynamics as well as use and usability of shared measures. This variable is based on two items that capture sufficient "financial resources" and "human resources" to get "work done effectively." In addition,

I account for the following three individual-level measures that may be associated with group members' perceptions of the dependent and independent variables: members' experience with work in collaborative settings, which ranges between not at all (1) and very often (5). A different variable captures whether (1) or not (0) a person is a founding member of their collaborative. Finally, I measure the extent to which members were involved in the group activities using a slider that ranges between "attended some meetings" and "involved in all decision-making."

A second modeling choice is the use of group fixed effects. These are important because they capture all factors unique to a group that were not specified in the model. They also account for the fact that responses from members of the same group are likely to be correlated, and they allow for some anchoring of the responses. A third choice I made is the use of different specifications, as shown in Table 4. Essentially, I opted for an approach where I add and compare the effects stepwise to account for the fact that the main variables of interest may be at least modestly correlated, allowing me to balance the risk of over- or under-specifying the models. I address these issues in my modeling as follows: I only use the controls, the group fixed effects, and those variables that are the least correlated with all others as baselevel predictors across the models. To examine the impact of all other factors, I include those only individually in one specification at a time (models 3–6) but finally present models that include as many variables as possible without running into multicollinearity issues (models 7–9).

Table 4 shows the results from the regression analysis. The "empty" model (1) that only includes the control variables and group fixed effects accounts for about 30 percent of the variation in shared measures use, while this percentage in all other models that include at least one other variable of main interest increases roughly up to 50 percent. What this suggests is that, overall, the factors I theorized about earlier in Section 3 do help improve our understanding of shared measures use. However, there is more nuance to this observation.

The impact of the egalitarian structures is mixed at best. A consensual decision-making style does foster use, but configurations where discussions are dominated by just a few or the existence of a more traditional top-down structure have little impact. Value congruence facilitates data use, but among all effects, this one has the smallest coefficient (model 6, standardized beta $= 0.30**$), which becomes insignificant once additional variables capturing other group dynamics are accounted for (model 9). The most crucial impact factors are group composition, social relationships, and distributed leadership. In addition to achieving statistical significance across-the-board, their coefficients roughly range between quarter and half of a standard deviation change in

Table 4 Explaining shared measures use (stepwise regressions)

	(1)	(2)	(3)	(4)	(5)	(6)	(7)	(8)	(9)
Egalitarian structure									
Top-Down structure (r)		0.08	0.04	0.05	0.08	0.09	0.03	0.05	0.04
		(0.347)	(0.642)	(0.519)	(0.294)	(0.281)	(0.672)	(0.503)	(0.576)
Dominated by a few (r)		−0.18^	−0.09	0.02	0.07	−0.08	0.01	0.07	−0.07
		(0.060)	(0.290)	(0.858)	(0.454)	(0.390)	(0.952)	(0.422)	(0.425)
Consensus		0.33**	0.21*	0.21*	0.13	0.26**	0.17*	0.09	0.20*
		(0.001)	(0.020)	(0.019)	(0.166)	(0.007)	(0.048)	(0.314)	(0.027)
Group composition			0.41**				0.26*	0.28**	0.36**
			(0.000)				(0.014)	(0.003)	(0.001)
Social relationships				0.46**			0.30*		
				(0.000)			(0.010)		
Distributed leadership					0.59**			0.47**	
					(0.000)			(0.000)	
Value congruence						0.30**			0.10
						(0.004)			(0.410)
Controls	Yes	Yes	Yes	Yes	Yes	Yes	Yes	Yes	Yes

Table 4 (cont.)

	(1)	(2)	(3)	(4)	(5)	(6)	(7)	(8)	(9)
Group fixed effects	Yes	Yes	Yes	Yes	Yes	Yes	Yes	Yes	Yes
N	126	119	119	119	116	119	119	116	119
R^2	0.327	0.461	0.550	0.553	0.575	0.504	0.579	0.612	0.553

Note: Standardized beta coefficients; p-values in parentheses; Ordinary least squares regressions. The dependent variable is a factor score consisting of the items listed in Table 3. Control variables are resources, experience, being a founding member, and involvement. Data: Main survey (Part 2).
$^\wedge$ p < 0.1, * p < 0.05, **p < 0.01

shared measures use, which can be considered fairly substantial (see models 7–8 in particular).

Here, to further substantiate and better understand these findings, I provide additional insights from the interviews. To better illustrate, I will begin by contrasting groups A and B that were introduced in Figure 5 earlier. Recall that group A was generally doing well in terms of its use of shared measures, while group B was struggling. The following illustrates the extent to which group A's dynamics appear to be more functional than those of group B, thereby confirming the quantitative findings from the aforementioned. In particular, interview results support that differences across groups regarding social relationships and distributed leadership are more prominent compared to group composition or value congruence.

Group A can be considered fairly diverse in terms of the roles and professions of its members and the organizations represented. As one group member put it, "having been able to involve even some of the agencies that historically don't get along with each other has been a significant win." Another group member stated that this is "probably a more diverse group than I have ever been a part of." One way through which group composition facilitated shared measures use is that the group intentionally and systematically tried to engage stakeholders as group members who may be able to help with getting access to relevant data.

In terms of social relationships, group A can be considered as a team whose members worked well together. Its members emphasized the importance of trust as a catalyst for effective communication, suggesting that being able to talk openly to people is important, but that such exchanges become more meaningful if a baselevel of trust has been established among members: "I can have open lines of communication with lots of people, but I don't necessarily trust what they are telling me." Group members considered their relationships sustainable over time but acknowledged that the group still had to prove that it truly created collective impact (that is, convince others it has an impact beyond that of a single agency or organization) in order to sustain the newly created network.

Group A showed signs of distributed leadership. While their leadership team was strong, active, and "in charge," members had opportunities to step-up. Particularly, the intermediate echelon – the subject-matter work groups – allowed members to take on responsibility regarding operating and coordinating a subgroup. Another example was that the group rotated participants for the SOG forums to allow many different members to be a part of these meetings in which groups were encouraged to engage in leadership tasks such as planning, organizing, and evaluating. As one trainer described it:

> They [the leadership team] are not just keeping a core group of people who
> are like "the primary" involved, they are really focused on ensuring that
> multiple members of that team get to experience this first-hand [participation
> in the SOG forums] . . . they have really been focused on spreading that love
> through members of the community group . . . . I would say they are very
> inclusive, and the core leadership group is highly respected and appreciated
> by the entire community group.

In my interviews with group A, references to shared values were scarce.
While this could be a sign that this was a less crucial factor – and, hence, would
confirm the quantitative findings – I would caution against drawing such
premature conclusions. Since this group had experienced little conflict with
respect to the definition of shared values or a joint purpose at the beginning of
the team building process, related issues may simply have taken up less time at
the stage at which I interviewed them.

The description of group B is different. While this group was not much less
diverse than group A, the stakeholder mix was not well represented by the
leadership team. The group's communication had been characterized as prob-
lematic. New members had a difficult time figuring out who to talk to in order to
get started, while current members did little to reach out to get the new members
onboard. The community group was likely to remain functional, but at a low
level of engagement and based on intra-group relationships that tended to be
underdeveloped.

Group B showed little evidence of distributed leadership. Knowledge was
very centralized, and I did come across an example of a member who wanted to
become more involved but essentially was told to "stay in her lane." Members
of the community group were kept in the loop rather than being engaged by the
leadership team. Such issues may have been amplified by the fact that strong
personalities and turnover among key personnel created tensions and challenges. Group B's members and their organizations did have sufficient capacity
to do impactful work, but their contributions have been described as siloed. One
trainer's assessment was that the group does share important values, but that
engaging in true collaboration was not necessarily one of them: "I think they
share value around what's best for the community, but they don't value that the
sum is greater than the individual parts."

The quantitative findings showed that an egalitarian structure was less influential than expected, with only one out of three measures having a positive
impact on data use. To better make sense of this finding, I draw on the qualitative insights into the dynamics within groups A and B. It is interesting to note
that both groups have been described as fairly hierarchical in the sense that there
is a clear distinction between the leadership team and the larger community

group when it comes to planning, coordinating, and decision-making. While less hierarchical than the traditional bureaucracy, neither group fits the description of being truly egalitarian. Yet, both groups used their hierarchical structures in very different ways. In group A, hierarchy was utilized to create structures that facilitated progress toward the shared goals, while encouraging bottom-up participation; whereas in group B, hierarchy led to the creation of echelons that co-existed independently, with neither a strong top-down nor bottom-up direction.

In group A, the leadership team was identified as an asset. The team set the agenda and pushed the community group forward, and it made sure the group was on track to meeting the requirements of the SOG training program. At the same time, the leadership team encouraged participation and tried to get as many members actively involved in decision-making processes. This was different for the leadership team of group B, which seemed to be disconnected from the larger community group. Rather than trying to involve the group as a whole, the leadership team here was trying to manage using a more centralized approach. Another trainer recalled a conversation between the team and the SOG trainers as follows:

> "This is what we [the leadership team] do." We were like, "How about group input?" They are like, "We know what we are doing." [I said:] "What about taking this back to the group?" [They said:] "That's fine. We'll tell them what we decided."

Another issue was that the group was constrained by the weaknesses of a hierarchical approach without leveraging its strengths. The missing opportunities for decentralization and bottom-up involvement were certainly such a weakness. Because of this, group members and their organizations remained underutilized, and the group lacked a clear sense of team. At the same time, the hierarchical structure did not yield more constructive formalization via protocols or explicit rules that could have helped better manage and coordinate the group, as one trainer described:

> "I don't think there was something like "this is what the leadership group is; here are our expectations" ... I don't think there were structure or mechanisms around consistency. You know, "let's talk about how we're going to deal with difference or group dynamics or conflict as a leadership team" .... Some of that formalization would have been helpful.

In addition to the insights from groups A and B, there are other noteworthy observations that came out of the focus groups and interviews with all ten groups. A central one is at the intersection of group structure and composition. As illustrated before, most groups had created some sort of a hierarchical structure, although members acknowledged that the structure of the opioid-response collaboratives tended to be much "flatter" than what they had experienced in their home organizations or previous multi-agency efforts. Sometimes, group-internal and -external hierarchies were incongruent, which became apparent when high-ranking members – often department or agency heads who, however, only got involved from time to time – tried to dominate the community meetings they attended. This behavior was not appreciated by regular group members.

Furthermore, the diversity of the groups did not seem to have significantly increased conflicts among members, despite different backgrounds, priorities, and perspectives. Most examples of conflicts dated back to times when the groups were newly created and involved discussions about vision and goals. For the most part, however, such conflicts were resolved as members spent more time working together and built trust. So, while fairly diverse and modestly hierarchical, most groups were hardly "political" – that is, they were not dominated by adversarial discussions in which participants were separated along lines that reflected membership in different organizations or policy networks.

This may have been achieved because, unlike in other more bureaucratic coordination efforts, membership in the opioid-response collaboratives was voluntary, and members subscribed to the primacy of a single joint purpose. Furthermore, developing social relationships and trust via working together for an extended period of time helped build bridges across professions and agencies. In that sense, understanding why public health and law enforcement professionals took on different perspectives when discussing opioid-related issues helped "debias" conversations about the meaning of performance data.

4.4 Culture, Shared Measures, and Nonroutine Feedback

So far, I have not examined the role of culture. I identified a "group culture" – as opposed to developmental, rational, or bureaucratic cultures – that is likely to be impactful. To further explore this hypothesis, I draw on a different survey (One-Page Survey, Forum 3). This survey was fielded during one of the training sessions that about fifty members from all ten groups attended. That survey employed three measures of group culture (all details are provided in the Appendix). One captures the construct directly and asks about the extent to which the "group is just like one big family" (adapted from Moynihan & Pandey, 2007). The other two items tap into the criteria that, according to the competing values framework (Cameron & Quinn, 2011), measure group culture: being flexible and internally focused. One item is about "cohesion and strong group-internal loyalty and ties," whereas the other item captures "flexibility and improvisation."

Surprisingly, all three measures of group culture are not strongly correlated, which is why I can examine their relative effects simultaneously. I also control for the impact of some of the group dynamics tested before, specifically items that capture the decision-making structure, group composition, trust, and value congruence (the wording of all items can be found in the Appendix) as well as group fixed effects. The dependent variable is a factor score of the usefulness (rather than the use) of shared measures because these data were collected when the groups were still in the process of developing measures. The three items, which make up the factor, cover purposes for the use of shared measures related to management, communication, and creating accountability (the exact items are listed in the note below Table 5).

Table 5 shows the results: two measures of group culture are not significant at all, whereas the third one ("group-internal loyalties and ties") shows an unexpected negative sign. Among the controls, items related to group composition ("need every member") and value congruence are significant, but those on the

Table 5 Group culture attributes and shared measures usefulness

Dominated by a few	0.28 (0.110)
Need every member	0.33* (0.033)
Trust	−0.08 (0.683)
Value congruence	0.43* (0.043)
Group culture	
"One big family"	0.05 (0.804)
"Group-Internal Loyalty and Ties"	−0.34^ (0.087)
"Flexibility and Improvisation"	−0.19 (0.248)
Controls	No
Group fixed effects	Yes
N	48
R^2	0.467

Note: Standardized beta coefficients; p-values in parentheses; Ordinary least squares regressions. The dependent variable is a factor score consisting of the following three items: Our goals, objectives, and measures are useful to ... manage our projects and resources more effectively; explain the value of what we do to others; and create accountability regarding what we accomplish. Data: One-Page Survey (Forum 3).
^ $p < 0.1$, * $p < 0.05$, ** $p < 0.01$

decision structure ("dominated by a few") and trust are not. Thus far, the findings show no evidence for the importance of a group culture for facilitating the collaboratives' work with shared measures.

To be able to better gauge the effect of group culture relative to other types of culture, I return to the Main Survey (Part 2). This survey includes four single items that tap into basic cultural differences across groups derived from the competing values framework. They include a focus on "resourcefully getting our work done" (rational), "having clear processes to accomplish our work" (bureaucratic), "creativity in accomplishing our work" (developmental), and "a strong collective identity to drive our work results" (group). Survey participants were asked to rank these culture descriptions regarding their accurateness in characterizing their respective collaborative from one to four (responses were provided by a subsample).

Other than introducing the culture items, my modeling here is similar to that in Table 4. The dependent variable is the use of shared measures (a factor score based on the items listed in Table 3), and I employ the same controls and group fixed effects as before. Since the ratings of all culture items are not independent from each other (only one type can be ranked 1, another 2, etc.), including all culture measures would over-specify the model. Hence, I leave group culture out of the model and use it as the reference category against which I contrast all other coefficients.

Table 6 shows the results: there is virtually no difference between the effect of a group and a rational culture. Interestingly, shared measures use is more likely

Table 6 Impact of culture on shared measures use

Type of culture (Reference: Group)	
Rational	0.01 (0.950)
Bureaucratic	0.21 (0.121)
Developmental	0.23^ (0.076)
Controls	Yes
Group fixed effects	Yes
N	70
R^2	0.605

Note: Unstandardized coefficients; p-values in parentheses; Ordinary least squares regressions. The dependent variable is a factor score consisting of the items listed in Table 3. Control variables are resources, experience, being a founding member, and involvement. Data: Main Survey (Part 2) (Subsample).
^ $p < 0.1$, * $p < 0.05$, ** $p < 0.01$

in the context of a bureaucratic rather than a group culture, although the p-value for this effect is above the 10 percent level. The clearest contrast is between a developmental and a group culture, in that the former fosters shared measures use relatively more, and this effect is significant. Overall, these findings run counter to my group-culture hypothesis. Thus, while culture may matter, it is not a strong group culture that facilitates collective data use.

As discussed before, shared measures are similar to organizational performance metrics, in that they are a part of regular, systematic control routines where data are collected after-the-fact based on predefined goals and indicators. However, this does not include nonroutine performance feedback that is often collected on the spot, which can be ad hoc, episodic, or verbal. Previous research has argued that only focusing on performance data, while ignoring all other nonroutine feedback, will paint an incomplete picture (Kroll, 2013; Tantardini, 2019). Sometimes public managers substitute the use of performance data with alternative means of nonroutine feedback. In fact, Mintzberg, in his classic 1975 piece, argued that aggregated, routine data produced via backward-looking management information systems are often inferior to ad hoc feedback that comes from other sources, including verbal media, calls, and meetings. So, while shared measures belong to the category of routine data, fully understanding how collaboratives work requires incorporating the use of nonroutine feedback in our analysis as well.

In another survey, which was conducted at the beginning of the project (Main Survey, Part 1), I asked group members about their use of nonroutine feedback. Specifically, I posed a question about the extent to which members "anticipate looking for feedback from the following actors about the impact of the collaborative and the achievement of its goals." The results are shown in Table 7, which factor analyzes the responses. Interestingly, as the factor loadings in that table suggest, responses about information-seeking preferences can be lumped into three alternative latent constructs. Some members tended to reach out to the civil society, others to decision-makers or professionals, respectively.

To better understand tendencies in seeking out different sources of nonroutine feedback, I examine the determinants of such behavior. Feedback seeking from the civil society, decision-makers, or professionals is operationalized via factor scores based on the item structure displayed in Table 7. To capture different group dynamics, I employ the variables group composition, egalitarian structure, and social relationships, which are measured the same way as in my previous analysis mentioned earlier (the exact wording of all items and scale reliabilities can be found in the Appendix). In short, group composition is based on perceptions of the group's diversity and the adequateness of the member selection. An

Table 7 Factor analysis of nonroutine feedback seeking

Feedback source	Civil society	Decision-makers	Professionals
Elected officials		0.863	
County managers		0.896	
Municipal managers		0.856	
Interest groups/Nonprofits	0.569		
Affected families	0.871		
Local residents	0.833		
Local media	0.768		
Researchers and experts			0.708
Healthcare agencies			0.793
Judicial system			0.820
Eigenvalues	4.483	1.491	1.004

Note: Principal component factoring was applied. Blanks represent factor loadings below 0.4. Items were measured using a five-point scale. Data: Main Survey (Part 1), n= 149. Survey question: "To what extent do you anticipate looking for feedback from the following actors about the impact of the collaborative and the achievement of its goals?"

egalitarian structure taps into consensus-oriented decision processes, whereas social relationships measure the quality of the communication and work relations among members. Just as before, I use group-level fixed effects and control for variables that may affect perceptions of the independent and dependent variables. Such factors include whether members represent an organization (1) or serve in their capacity as community members (0), whether (1) or not (0) members have worked before with each other, and whether members have worked in collaborative settings before (1 = not at all; 5 = very often).

Table 8 shows the regression results. Overall, the consensus structure plays a minor role, and there is some overlap and some differences between the effects of group composition and social relationships. Both variables are associated with reaching out to professionals to collect nonroutine feedback. However, high scores on the group composition index are more related to outreach to the civil society ($\beta = 0.16^{\wedge}$), while good social relationships within the group are more correlated with seeking feedback from decision-makers ($\beta = 0.24^{**}$). These findings, along with all others presented in this section, will be discussed in the next subsection.

Table 8 Explaining nonroutine feedback seeking

	Civil society		Decision-makers		Professionals	
	(1)	(2)	(3)	(4)	(5)	(6)
Group composition	0.16^ (0.071)		0.12 (0.167)		0.18* (0.035)	
Social relationships		0.12 (0.173)		0.24** (0.009)		0.19* (0.033)
Consensus structure	−0.01 (0.941)	−0.02 (0.856)	0.06 (0.486)	0.00 (0.979)	0.15^ (0.065)	0.12 (0.156)
Controls	Yes	Yes	Yes	Yes	Yes	Yes
Group fixed effects	Yes	Yes	Yes	Yes	Yes	Yes
N	147	148	147	148	147	148
R^2	0.174	0.176	0.168	0.199	0.229	0.229

Note: Standardized beta coefficients; p-values in parentheses; Ordinary least squares regressions. The dependent variables are factor scores consisting of the items listed in Table 7. Control variables are organization representative, past relations, and experience. Data: Main Survey (Part 1).

^ $p < 0.1$, * $p < 0.05$, ** $p < 0.01$

4.5 Discussion of the Findings

Some of the basic findings regarding the use of shared measures in collaborations are consistent with what we know about performance data use more broadly (Kroll, 2015a; Moynihan & Pandey, 2010). Shared measures are used to inform decision-making, but there is no linear connection between the data and specific decision outcomes. In some instances, data will be considered, but they might only be indirectly linked to decisions or result in not being influential at all. By and large, this confirms what we know about performance information use in the public sector, where decision-relevant data are rarely collected in real time and the use of sophisticated data centers are the exception.

Data use in collaborations can be more or less collective. While in theory, collaboratives are best positioned to employ shared measures as the basis for negotiated use among equal partners, some collaborations may instead rely on existing agency data, or decisions could be driven by single organizations (see Douglas & Ansell, 2021). This may have to do, in part, with the fact that data issues are particularly pronounced for the use of shared measures. In fact, using existing agency data will often be easier than identifying and integrating shared measures across organizations, jurisdictions, and formats. But the effective use of shared measures also requires the right group dynamics, as the following paragraphs will illustrate.

Relational factors matter. One general question that this Element has been advancing is whether data use in collaborations can be explained by mechanisms other than those featured in the traditional performance management literature. Consequently, the answer seems to be "yes." Generally, the theoretical perspectives put forward in Section 3, which were inspired by a stewardship (not agency) approach, and which featured group-centered concepts such as social exchange and collective norms and values, help us better understand shared measures use.

One relevant factor is high-quality social relationships (Banks et al., 2014; Nahapiet & Ghoshal, 1998). This is because such relationships foster data use through developing trust, which makes it easier to exchange and discuss information and lowers the transactions costs of this process. It is possible for groups that have developed quality relationships among members to coordinate and manage tasks via social mechanisms as opposed to data systems, but the findings of this study do not confirm such behavior. Instead, social capital seems to be compatible with shared measures, maybe because working with shared measures – as opposed to other types of performance data – is an effort that often mirrors effective group processes.

Distributed leadership is another central concept (Bolden, 2011; Zhu et al., 2018). Its value becomes particularly clear when contrasted with an egalitarian structure, which was discovered to be less impactful. Collaborations that subscribe to an egalitarian decision-making mode value the participation of, and consensus among, a large majority of members. While this can be important for the inclusion of as much intellectual capital as possible, a pure consensus focus can also yield inefficiencies and stagnation. Hence, some hierarchical structures may be needed to leverage seemingly bureaucratic benefits such as specialization, predictability, and articulated lines of communication. Essentially, a balance needs to be struck between participatory decision-making and efficiency. Distributed leadership could be combined with either egalitarian or semi-hierarchical structures. What is important here is that – beyond being involved in the decision-making – most group members need to be able to take on leadership roles, including organizing, problem solving, or providing moral support to fellow members.

Group diversity and value congruence also facilitate shared measures use, albeit to a lesser degree. With respect to group composition and diversity, it is interesting that previous research lends itself to the formulation of two alternative hypotheses: on one hand, diversity may yield conflict that could harm purposeful use, whereas on the other hand, diversity may be needed to generate new ideas and balance opinions (Duchek et al., 2020; Moynihan, 2008). Findings from the case suggest that the influence on performance data use is positively reinforcing, not harming. Essentially, creativity effects seem to outweigh conflict, and the latter – if moderated well – can be productive, too. Overall, there was little evidence across groups that politicization due to fragmented interests would significantly undermine purposeful use.

The value-congruence effect was also modestly positive, a finding that requires some further elaboration. Value congruence is known to help develop a joint cognitive frame that facilitates collective sensemaking processes (Edwards & Cable, 2009; Mohammed et al., 2010). At the same time, even in a well-managed collaborative, members representing different organizations from different sectors may not need to fully share the same values as long as they work toward a joint purpose. Notwithstanding such qualifications, shared values can give legitimacy to performance data, particularly if the latter are used to capture achievements of goals and priorities that are equally valued by most group members.

Understanding how collaborations respond to performance information also requires considering feedback sources other than shared measures (Kroll, 2013; Tantardini, 2019). Groups preferred reaching out to three potential sources of informal, nonroutine feedback: members of the civil society, decision makers, and professionals. While, generally, members tended to reach out to professionals, group diversity was linked to outreach to the civil society, whereas effective social relationships were associated with seeking out decision-makers. It seems to make sense that diverse groups appreciate bottom-up grassroot input at the societal level where it is most widely available through nonprofits, affected families, residents, or the media. In contrast, well developed relationships among group members likely spillover into relational networks outside of the group, involving elected officials and managers. What this suggests is that group dynamics do not just explain shared measures use but may also trigger divergent patterns of more general feedback-seeking behavior, an observation that certainly calls for additional research.

Nonetheless, all findings are subject to limitations. For one, the null findings around the culture variables may be at least partially driven by some degree of measurement error. The items used to capture the construct should be understood as proxies, which is why future research needs to replicate the findings using more comprehensive scales. Despite such issues, however, different analyses using differently focused items from different surveys yielded the same conclusion: culture – and, specifically, a group or clan culture – was not much related to shared measures use. A second concern might be related to potential common-source bias. That is, although multiple surveys were used, the data for both sides of each regression equation were drawn from the same instrument. But this problem was mitigated by additional interviews with group members and trainers as well as a document review that helped triangulate the findings.

In addition, generalizations from the case study should be understood as theoretical and analytic, not as broader inferences to a specific population. Along these lines, the goal was to establish causalities within the case and embed these findings in broader theory to extract more generalizable causal mechanisms. In that sense, as Yin (2013) has pointed out before, single case studies are akin to field experiments conducted in a single organization: their focus is on cause and effect, rather than the representativeness of the sample. Generalizations may also be limited to some degree because in my case study, collaboratives were able to develop their performance practices mostly independently, whereas in other cases funders may be more actively involved in configuring a specific performance management framework.

5 Conclusion

Using the case of community-level opioid-response collaborations in North Carolina, I found that several relational group-centered factors mattered when explaining shared measures use. Social relationships and distributed leadership showed a significant impact, followed by group composition and value congruence, while egalitarian structures showed mixed findings, and a clan culture played no crucial role. This section draws out some conclusions for theory and research and makes several recommendations for public management practice.

5.1 Implications for Research

This Element began with the premise that performance practices in collaborations are likely to differ in nature from practices in hierarchical agency settings. It then theorized and examined the role of relational, stewardship-inspired factors, which were mostly disregarded in organizational performance management research. It found overall support for their relevance in explaining the collective use of shared measures. My research into the determinants of collective use should be understood as a first step, with much space for future research. In addition to studying other relational factors, future research could compare the relative impact or interactions of relational and conventional explanation factors, such as data visualization choices, differences in measurement systems, or individual-level member attributes (James et al., 2020; Kroll, 2015a).

Some of the findings made in a collaborative setting might be transferable back to the original agency context. Theories of performance information use acknowledged early on that such behavior should be understood as a social process (Moynihan, 2008; Van Dooren & Van den Walle, 2008). That is, data use can rarely be described as one individual responding to a performance stimulus. Rather, multiple individuals via interactions among themselves and through dialogue routines make sense of data that might, in a second step, inform the individual's decision-making. If data use, even in bureaucratic organizations, is more collaborative than often assumed, then some of the factors examined in this Element may also be relevant to further enhance organization-centric performance management theories. A second implication is methodological: to account for the fact that performance information use might be best modeled as a collective, social process, experimental designs may want to move beyond scenarios where a respondent reacts to a piece of performance information. Instead, experiments could create virtual spaces where multiple respondents are confronted with performance data and, through multiple, guided rounds of interactions, engage in a joint sensemaking process.

An alternative approach to better get at the core of collective data use behavior is through social network analysis. Data use could be modeled via discussion networks of performance information that are based on contacts people talk to about performance data. Social network analysis could then be employed to explain differences in the probabilities of tie formation between pairs of individuals for the purpose of data-informed decision-making. This approach could contribute to further enhancing our understanding of data use in organizations but even more so in cross-organizational collaborations. Another way to study collective use, which is most suitable for the collaborative setting, is via information aggregation at the group level. Particularly, if the purpose is to examine collective use based on a high number of long-standing collaboratives and repeated measures over time, central variables could be aggregated at the collaboration-level or examined through multi-level techniques.

A final avenue for future research is taking a longitudinal perspective, which would allow tracking changes in crucial variables over multiple years. This Element examined the role of trust, but it was neither able to precisely distinguish between groups with higher or lower baselevels of trust among community members prior to joining the collaborative. Nor was it fully able to dissect the impact of increasing or decreasing trust effects over time on shared measures use. A second factor with a significant longitudinal relevance is the support for a collaborative by the top-level leaders of its most central member organizations. Collaboratives often have a difficult time retaining high-level interest, and they can easily run out of steam when they lose such support.

5.2 Recommendations for Practice

I will give some attention to the question of how the mechanisms, which I found to be drivers of shared measures use, can be created or activated. Before I do this, however, I will offer recommendations focused on collective use behavior more narrowly. To develop lessons for practice, I turn to observations from the case and reflect on their potential for facilitating data use in collaborations more broadly.

Prioritize organization-spanning goals. Agency representatives' mindsets are configured in ways that make them think through problems using an organization-centered prism. Often, what members know, based on experiences from organizations, also shapes their behavior in collaborative settings. It is therefore not uncommon that a collaboration's priority list mirrors the individual objectives of their most powerful member organizations. However, such a list would be a missed opportunity. When writing goals, collaborations should prioritize objectives whose achievement requires multiple organizations to work together. After all, collaborations will have the most impact when they tackle problems that cannot be solved by a single organization.

Address data-integration issues head on. Collecting data on cross-cutting issues often requires integrating metrics that were recorded in different formats by several agencies, which can be difficult. Hence, to make this more feasible, choices for shared measures need to be practical. A simple measure that, however, allows regular data breakouts by type, group, or area can be superior to a complex metric for which it is difficult to collect any data. A strategy that can facilitate integration is to invite stakeholders, who may be gatekeepers for specific types of data, to become regular collaboration members.

Develop routines of data review. Each meeting should include a segment in which the group discusses data. This is a great way to track progress toward central goals and can direct discussions to areas that need attention. But it will also help group members learn how to make sense of data using benchmarks and other points of reference. In addition to reviewing trends based on shared measures, data segments could also be used to invite external speakers or review data that were most currently featured in the media or in members' professional networks. If a collaborative consists of multiple subgroups, each of which tracks their fair share of metrics, then regular data review sessions could be rotated by subgroup theme.

Try to debias discussions. Interpretations of data are driven by individual biases that are often a function of different values, roles, and experiences. Therefore, several people looking at the same data may draw very different conclusions. For example, low performance scores could allow for very different actions to be taken, including doing more of the same, abandoning the current approach, or increasing or cutting funds. If group members disagree on interpretations or actions because of different backgrounds (e.g., law enforcement versus public health), helping members understand why they disagree and showing them that a diversity of viewpoints can be productive may prevent overheated discussions. In fact, diverse collaborations are less likely to engage in groupthink and more likely to keep individual biases in check.

Create opportunities for leadership to become distributed. Shared leadership is not tied to formal roles and instead often emerges informally. However, some structural choices may help support efforts of distributed leadership among members. For example, structures based on multiple horizontally layered theme-based workgroups combined with some light vertical differentiation will create many positions for members to take on responsibility and lead. Additionally, groups can foster distributed leadership by rotating members through formal leadership positions or by asking for volunteers to take charge of singular projects or milestones. Along these lines, particular structural choices may reinforce existing shared leadership tendencies and nudge individuals to become more engaged in functions, such as planning, problem solving, or mentoring.

Make trust-building a priority from the start. Most efforts related to shared performance practices require groups to find and agree on joint goals and measures right at the onset. However, at that point, members rarely know each other, and trust levels tend to be low. Therefore, vision exercises and planning efforts often end up less productive than expected, and they can require a fair amount of mediation among conflicting interests. Ways to build trust early on include working in smaller subgroups consisting of individuals with prior connections. Additionally, retreats or excursions can be beneficial if their main function is to help members network and get to know each other, rather than engage in real strategic planning.

Leverage the benefits of group diversity and manage its challenges. Diverse groups can draw on various types of knowledge; furthermore, these views tend to be more balanced and make decision-making more creative. However, one important condition is that the group's diversity is reflected in its structure. That is, member diversity needs to be represented among work-group leaders and group coordinators. If the entire group is diverse but the leadership team only represents one or two organizations, it will be difficult to tap into the group's full diversity potential. Furthermore, to avoid that functional or demographic diversity yields unproductive conflicts, groups need to articulate a purpose and priorities that most members value. In such a light, shared mental models at the macro level can help overcome differences at the micro level.

You need both (top-down) structure and (bottom-up) participation. Most groups will likely benefit from a mix of broad inclusiveness as well as structured mechanisms that facilitate decision-making and progress. Of course, some of the most central benefits of collaborations are their horizontal, egalitarian features based on debate and consensus. Along these lines, egalitarian structures – once established – need to be protected against "outside interference." Sometimes high-ranking stakeholders, who are irregular group members, but emphasize their rank or role in the hierarchy when they show up, can undermine participatory decision-making practices. While such hierarchical power games are counterproductive, other types of structure such as the creation of a leadership or coordination team (vertical differentiation) as well as theme-driven work groups (horizontal differentiation) can be helpful.

Appreciate nonroutine feedback in addition to shared measures. While this Element has devoted most of its attention to shared measures and data, there is relevant performance feedback aside from the quantitative, formalized type. Hence, working with shared measures should not mean neglecting all other nonroutine performance input. Ideally, becoming comfortable with using shared goals, measures, and quantitative data should also make members more receptive to various kinds of mission-relevant feedback. Members need to embrace and leverage their group-external connections for that purpose. The fact that most collaborations consist of a heterogenous set of members will help multiply the number of their external feedback sources and reinforce the collaborative advantage over more traditional organizational settings.

Appendix

Measures across Surveys (Explanation Factors)

Factors	Main Survey (Part 1)	One-Page Survey (Forum 3)	Main Survey (Part 2)
Group Composition (Index)	• Our collaborative members represent a wide range of people and groups. • We have the right people and groups involved in our collaborative to be effective. ($\alpha = 0.75$; five-point scale)	• We need every member in our group to produce results.	• Our collaborative members represent a wide range of people and groups. • We have the right people and groups involved in our collaborative to be effective. ($\alpha = 0.88$; five-point scale)
Egalitarian Structure	• Consensus decision-making (dummy variable).	• Deliberations are dominated by a few people (reversed).	• Our collaborative has a top-down structure (reversed; five-point) • Discussions are dominated by a few people (reversed; five-point) • Consensus decision-making (dummy variable).
Social Relationships (Index)	• Overall, members of this collaborative work well together. • Our collaborative shares information effectively.	• There is a great deal of trust among all group members (trust).	• Overall, members of this collaborative work well together. • Our collaborative shares information effectively.

(cont.)

Factors	Main Survey (Part 1)	One-Page Survey (Forum 3)	Main Survey (Part 2)
	• Our collaborative members communicate well with each other. • Collaborative members trust each other. ($\alpha = 0.88$; five-point)	• Our collaborative members communicate well with each other. • Collaborative members trust each other. ($\alpha= 0.92$; 5-point)	
Distributed Leadership (Index)	—	—	In our collaborative, most members engage in the following activities: • Deciding how to go about our work. • Providing helpful input about collaborative's work plans. • Deciding on best course of action when problems arise. • Solving problems as they arise. • Providing support to collaborative members who need help. • Encouraging other collaborative members when they're upset.

| Culture | — | <ul><li>Our group is just like one big family.</li><li>Our collaborative is characterized by cohesion and strong group-internal loyalty and ties (opposite endpoint: our collaborative is characterized as a conglomerate of people with different interests).</li><li>Our collaborative works based on flexibility and improvisation (opposite endpoint: our collaborative is governed through formal principles and rules).</li></ul> | <ul><li>Helping to develop each other's skills</li><li>Being positive role models to new members of the collaborative. ($\alpha = 0.96$)</li><li>We focus on resourcefully getting our work done (rational).</li><li>We focus on having clear processes to accomplish our work (bureaucratic).</li><li>We focus on a strong collective identity to drive our work results (group).</li><li>We focus on creativity in accomplishing our work (developmental) (four-point ranking scale).</li></ul> |

(cont.)

Factors	Main Survey (Part 1)	One-Page Survey (Forum 3)	Main Survey (Part 2)
Value Congruence (Index)	—	• Group members share the same values.	• Collaborative members share the same values. • Collaborative members are able to answer "why" our collaborative is needed. ($\alpha = 0.82$; five-point)

Note: α = Cronbach's Alpha. All items were measured using seven-point scales, unless otherwise listed.

References

Agranoff, R. (2007). *Managing within networks: Adding value to public organizations*. Washington, DC: Georgetown University Press.

Amirkhanyan, A., Kim, H., & Lambright, K. (2012). Closer than "arm's length": Understanding the factors associated with collaborative contracting. *American Review of Public Administration*, 42(3), 341–366.

Ammons, D. (2020). *Performance measurement for managing local government: Getting it right*. Irvine, CA: Melvin and Leigh.

Ammons, D., & Rivenbark, W. (2008). Factors influencing the use of performance data to improve municipal services: Evidence from the North Carolina benchmarking project. *Public Administration Review*, 68(2), 304–318.

Amos, O. (2017). Why opioids are such an American problem. BBC News. www.bbc.com/news/world-us-canada–41701718.

Andersen, S., & Moynihan, D. (2016). How leaders respond to diversity: The moderating role of organizational culture on performance information use. *Journal of Public Administration Research and Theory*, 26(3), 448–460.

Askim, J., Bjurstrøm, K., & Kjærvik, J. (2019). Quasi-contractual ministerial steering of state agencies: Its intensity, modes, and how agency characteristics matter. *International Public Management Journal*, 22(3), 470–498.

Baekgaard, M., Christensen, J., Dahlmann, C., Mathiasen, A., & Petersen, N. (2019). The role of evidence in politics: Motivated reasoning and persuasion among politicians. *British Journal of Political Science*, 49(3), 1117–1140.

Banks, G., Batchelor, J., Seers, A., O'Boyle, E., Pollack, J., & Gower, K. (2014). What does team–member exchange bring to the party? A meta-analytic review of team and leader social exchange. *Journal of Organizational Behavior*, 35(2), 273–295.

Behn, R. (2003). Why measure performance? Different purposes require different measures. *Public Administration Review*, 63(5), 586–606.

Behn, R. (2014). *The PerformanceStat potential: A leadership strategy for producing results*. Washington, DC: Brookings Institution Press/Ash Center.

Belardinelli, P., Bellé, N., Sicilia, M., & Steccolini, I. (2018). Framing effects under different uses of performance information: An experimental study on public managers. *Public Administration Review*, 78(6), 841–851.

Benaine, S., & Kroll, A. (2020). Explaining effort substitution in performance systems: The role of task demands and mission orientation. *Public Management Review*, 22(6), 813–835.

Bjurstrøm, K. (2019). How interagency coordination is affected by agency policy autonomy. *Public Management Review*, 23(3), 397–421.

Bjurstrøm, K. (2020). Principal–agent or principal–steward: How ministry-agency relations condition the impact of performance management in the steering of government agencies. *Public Performance and Management Review*, 43(5), 1053–1077.

Black, J., & Gregersen, H. (1997). Participative decision-making: An integration of multiple dimensions. *Human Relations*, 50(7), 859–878.

Bohte, J., & Meier, K. (2000). Goal displacement: Assessing the motivation for organizational cheating. *Public Administration Review*, 60(2), 173–182.

Bolden, R. (2011). Distributed leadership in organizations: A review of theory and research. *International Journal of Management Reviews*, 13(3), 251–269.

Brown, T., Potoski, M., & Van Slyke, D. (2006). Managing public service contracts: Aligning values, institutions, and markets. *Public Administration Review*, 66(3), 323–331.

Bryson, J., Crosby, B., & Stone, M. (2006). The design and implementation of cross-sector collaborations: Propositions from the literature. *Public Administration Review*, 66(1), 44–55.

Bryson, J., Crosby, B., & Stone, M. (2015). Designing and implementing cross-sector collaborations: Needed and challenging. *Public Administration Review*, 75(5), 647–663.

Calciolari, S., Prenestini, A., & Lega, F. (2018). An organizational culture for all seasons? How cultural type dominance and strength influence different performance goals. *Public Management Review*, 20(9), 1400–1422.

Cameron, K., & Quinn, R. (2011). *Diagnosing and changing organizational culture: Based on the competing values*. San Francisco, CA: Wiley.

Centers of Disease Control and Preventions (CDC). (2021a). Opioid overdose. www.cdc.gov/drugoverdose/epidemic/index.html.

Centers of Disease Control and Preventions (CDC). (2021b). U.S. opioid dispensing rate maps. www.cdc.gov/drugoverdose/maps/rxrate-maps.html.

Chen, Z. (2018). A literature review of team-member exchange and prospects. *Journal of Service Science and Management*, 11(4), 433–454.

Choi, S., Kim, K., & Kang, S.-W. (2017). Effects of transformational and shared leadership styles on employees' perception of team effectiveness. *Social Behavior and Personality*, 45(3), 377–386.

Choi, I., & Moynihan, D. (2019). How to foster collaborative performance management? Key factors in the US federal agencies. *Public Management Review*, 21(10), 1538–1559.

Christensen, J., Dahlmann, C., Mathiasen, A., Moynihan, D., & Petersen, N. (2018). How do elected officials evaluate performance? Goal preferences, governance preferences, and the process of goal reprioritization. *Journal of Public Administration Research and Theory*, 28(2), 197–211.

Cotton, J., Vollrath, D., Froggatt, K., Lengnick-Hall, M., & Jennings, K. (1988). Employee participation: Diverse forms and different outcomes. *Academy of Management Review*, 13(1), 8–22.

Cummings, J. (2004). Work groups, structural diversity, and knowledge sharing in a global organization. *Management Science*, 50(3), 352–364.

Davis, J., Schoorman, F., & Donaldson, L. (1997). Toward a stewardship theory of management. *Academy of Management Review*, 22(1), 20–47.

Dee, T., & Jacob, B. (2011). The impact of No Child Left Behind on student achievement. *Journal of Policy Analysis and Management*, 30(3), 418–446.

Denhardt, K., & Aristigueta, M. (2008). Performance management system: Providing accountability and challenging collaboration. In: W. Van Dooren & S. Van de Walle (Eds.), *Performance information on the public sector: How it is used* (pp. 106–122). Basingstoke: Palgrave Macmillan.

Dermer, J., & Lucas, R. (1986). The illusion of managerial control. *Accounting, Organizations and Society*, 11(6), 471–482.

Doberstein, C. (2016). Designing collaborative governance decision-making in search of a "collaborative advantage." *Public Management Review*, 18(6), 819–841.

Douglas, M. (1996). *Natural symbols: Explorations in cosmology*. London: Routledge.

Douglas, S., & Ansell, C. (2021). Getting a grip on the performance of collaborations: Examining collaborative performance regimes and collaborative performance summits. *Public Administration Review*, 81(5), 951–961.

Douglas, J., Raudla, R., Randma-Liiv, T., & Savi, R. (2019). The impact of greater centralization on the relevance of performance information in European governments during the fiscal crisis. *Administration and Society*, 51(7), 1020–1050.

Duchek, S., Raetze, S., & Scheuch, I. (2020). The role of diversity in organizational resilience: A theoretical framework. *Business Research*, 13, 387–423.

Dull, M. (2009). Results-model reform leadership: Questions of credible commitment. *Journal of Public Administration Research and Theory*, 19(2), 255–284.

Edwards, J., & Cable, D. (2009). The value of value congruence. *Journal of Applied Psychology*, 94(3), 654–677.

Eisenhardt, L. (1989). Agency theory: An assessment and review. *Academy of Management Review*, 14(1), 57–74.

Emerson, K., & Nabatchi, T. (2015a). *Collaborative governance regimes.* Washington, DC: Georgetown University Press.

Emerson, K., & Nabatchi, T. (2015b). Evaluating the productivity of collaborative governance regimes: A performance matrix. *Public Performance and Management Review,* 38(4), 717–747.

Emerson, K., Nabatchi, T., & Balogh, S. (2012). An integrative framework for collaborative governance. *Journal of Public Administration Research and Theory,* 22(1), 1–29.

Folz, D., Abdelrazek, R., & Chung, Y. (2009). The adoption, use, and impacts of performance measures in medium-size cities. *Public Performance and Management Review,* 33(1), 63–87.

Gagné, N., & Deci, E. (2005). Self-determination theory and work motivation. *Journal of Organizational Behavior,* 26(4), 331–362.

George, B., Baekgaard, M., Decramer, A., Audenaert, M., & Goeminne, S. (2020). Institutional isomorphism, negativity bias and performance information use by politicians: A survey experiment. *Public Administration,* 98(1), 14–28.

Gerrish, E. (2016). The impact of performance management on performance in public organizations: A meta-analysis. *Public Administration Review,* 76(1), 48–66.

Getha-Taylor, H. (2019). *Partnerships that last: Identifying the keys to resilient collaboration.* Cambridge, UK: Cambridge University Press.

Girth, A. (2014). A closer look at contract accountability: Exploring the determinants of sanctions for unsatisfactory contract performance. *Journal of Public Administration Research and Theory,* 24(2), 317–348.

Grissom, J. (2012). Revisiting the impact of participative decision making on public employee retention: The moderating influence of effective managers. *American Review of Public Administration,* 42(4), 400–418.

Gu, J., Chen, Z., Huang, Q., Liu, H., & Huang, S. (2018). A multilevel analysis of the relationship between shared leadership and creativity in inter-organizational teams. *Journal of Creative Behavior,* 52(2), 109–126.

Han, Y. (2020). The impact of accountability deficit on agency performance: Performance-accountability regime. *Public Management Review,* 22(6), 927–948.

Hatry, H. (2006). *Performance measurement: Getting results.* Washington, DC: The Urban Institute Press.

He, W., Hao, P., Huang, X., Long, L.-R., Hiller, N., & Li, S.-L. (2020). Different roles of shared and vertical leadership in promoting team creativity: Cultivating and synthesizing team members' individual creativity. *Personnel Psychology,* 73(1), 199–225.

Heinrich, C., & Marschke, G. (2010). Incentives and their dynamics in public sector performance management systems. *Journal of Policy Analysis and Management*, 29(1), 183–208.

Henderson, A., & Bromberg, D. (2015). Performance information use in local government: Monitoring relationships with emergency medical services agencies. *Public Performance and Management Review*, 39(1), 58–82.

Hiller, N., Day, D., & Vance, R. (2006). Collective enactment of leadership roles and team effectiveness: A field study. *Leadership Quarterly*, 17(4), 387–397.

Ho, A. (2006). Accounting for the value of performance measurement from the perspective of midwestern mayors. *Journal of Public Administration Research and Theory*, 16(2), 217–237.

Hodgson. G. (2006). What are institutions? *Journal of Economic Issues*, 40(1), 1–25.

Hoffman, J., & Benner, K. (2020). Purdue Pharma Pleads Guilty to Criminal Charges for Opioid Sales. New York Times. www.nytimes.com/2020/10/21/health/purdue-opioids-criminal-charges.html.

Hoffman, B., Bynum, B., Piccolo, R., & Sutton, A. (2011). Person-organization value congruence: How transformational leaders influence work group effectiveness. *Academy of Management Journal*, 54(4), 779–796.

Holm, J. (2017). Double standards? How historical and political aspiration levels guide managerial performance information use. *Public Administration*, 95(4), 1026–1040.

Holm, J. (2018). Successful problem solvers? Managerial performance information use to improve low organizational performance. *Journal of Public Administration Research and Theory*, 28(3), 303–320.

Hood. C. (2000). *The art of the state. Culture, rhetoric, and public management.* Oxford, UK: Oxford University Press.

Hood, C. (2012). Public management by numbers as a performance-enhancing drug: Two hypotheses. *Public Administration Review*, 72(S1), S85–S92.

Horwitz, S., & Horwitz, I. (2007). The effects of team diversity on team outcomes: A meta-analytic review of team demography. *Journal of Management*, 33(6), 987–1015.

Imperial, M. (2004). *Collaboration and performance management in network settings: Lessons from three watershed governance efforts.* Washington, DC: IBM Center for The Business of Government.

Isett, K., Mergel, I., LeRoux, K., Mischen, P., & Rethemeyer, R. (2011). Networks in public administration scholarship: Understanding where we are and where we need to go. *Journal of Public Administration Research and Theory*, 21(suppl_1), i157–i173.

Jager, N., Newig, J., Challies, E., & Kochskämper, E. (2020). Pathways to implementation: Evidence on how participation in environmental governance impacts on environmental outcomes. *Journal of Public Administration Research and Theory*, 30(3), 383–399.

Jakobsen, M., Baekgaard, M., Moynihan, D., & Loon, N. (2018). Making sense of performance regimes: Rebalancing external accountability and internal learning. *Perspectives on Public Management and Governance*, 1(2), 127–141.

James, O., Moynihan, D., Olsen, A., & Van Ryzin, G. (2020). *Behavioral public performance: How people make sense of government metrics*. Cambridge, UK: Cambridge University Press.

Janis, I. (1991). Groupthink. In: E. Griffin (Ed.), *A first look at communication theory* (pp. 235–246). New York: McGrawHill.

Jensen, M., & Meckling, W. (1976). Theory of the firm: Managerial behavior, agency costs and ownership structure. *Journal of Financial Economics*, 3(4), 305–360.

Johnston, E., Hicks, D., Nan, N., & Auer, J. (2011). Managing the inclusion process in collaborative governance. *Journal of Public Administration Research and Theory*, 21(4), 699–721.

Jones, M., Viswanath, O., Peck, J., Kaye, A, Gill, J., & Simopoulos, T. (2018). A brief history of the opioid epidemic and strategies for pain medicine. *Pain and Therapy*, 7, 13–21.

Kahan, D. (2016). The politically motivated reasoning paradigm, Part 1: What politically motivated reasoning is and how to measure it. *Emerging Trends in the Social and Behavioral Sciences*, https://doi.org/10.1002/9781118900772 .etrds0417.

Katz, J., & Sanger-Katz, M. (2021). "It's huge, it's historic, it's unheard-of": Drug overdose deaths spike. New York Times. www.nytimes.com/interactive/2021/07/14/upshot/drug-overdose-deaths.html.

Kettl, D. (2006). Managing boundaries in American administration: The collaboration imperative. *Public Administration Review*, 66(1), 10–19.

Kim, J., & Siddiki, S. (2018). Linking diversity of collaborative policymaking venues with procedural justice perceptions: A study of U.S. marine aquaculture partnerships. *American Review of Public Administration*, 48(2), 159–174.

King, E., Hebl, M., & Beal, D. (2009). Conflict and cooperation in diverse workgroups. *Journal of Social Issues*, 65(2), 261–285.

Kontopoulos, K. (1993). *The logics of social structure*. Cambridge, UK: Cambridge University Press

Krause, T., & Swiatczak, M. (2021). In control we trust!? Exploring formal control configurations for municipally owned corporations. *Journal of Public Budgeting, Accounting and Financial Management*, 33(3), 314–342.

Kristof-Brown, A., Zimmerman, R., & Johnson, E. (2005). Consequences of individuals' fit at work: A meta-analysis of person–job, person–organization, person–group, and person–supervisor fit. *Personnel Psychology*, 58(2), 281–342.

Kroll, A. (2013). The other type of performance information: Nonroutine feedback, its relevance and use. *Public Administration Review*, 73(2), 265–276.

Kroll, A. (2014). Why performance information use varies among public managers: Testing manager-related explanations. *International Public Management Journal*, 17(2), 174–201.

Kroll, A. (2015a). Drivers of performance information use: Systematic literature review and directions for future research. *Public Performance and Management Review*, 38(3), 459–486.

Kroll, A. (2015b). Explaining the use of performance information by public managers: A planned-behavior approach. *American Review of Public Administration*, 45(2): 201–215.

Kroll, A. (2021). Why you should care about shared measures. In: K. Nelson (Ed.), *Using the collective impact process as a model to address complex community problems: Lessons learned from the Opioid Response Project* (pp. 85–92). Chapel Hill, NC: School of Government at the University of North Carolina–Chapel Hill.

Kroll, A., DeHart-Davis, L., & Vogel, D. (2019). Mechanisms of social capital in organizations: How team cognition influences employee commitment and engagement. *American Review of Public Administration*, 49(7), 777–791.

Kroll, A., & Moynihan, D. (2018). The design and practice of integrating evidence: connecting performance management with program evaluation. *Public Administration Review*, 78(2), 183–194.

Kroll, A., & Moynihan, D. (2021). Tools of control? Comparing congressional and presidential performance management reforms. *Public Administration Review*, 81(4), 599–609.

Kroll, A., & Vogel, D. (2014). The PSM-leadership fit: A model of performance information use. *Public Administration*, 92(4), 974–991.

Kroll, A., & Vogel, D. (2021). Why public employees manipulate performance data: Prosocial impact, job stress, and red tape. *International Public Management Journal*, 24(2), 164–182.

Leach, D. (2016). When freedom is not an endless meeting: A new look at efficiency in consensus-based decision making. *Sociological Quarterly*, 57 (1), 36–70.

Leana, C., & Van Buren, H. (1999). Organizational social capital and employment practices. *Academy of Management Review*, 24(3), 538–555.

Lee, J. (2018). The opioid crisis is a wicked problem. *American Journal on Addictions*, 27(1), 51.

Lee, S., Park, J.-G., & Lee, J. (2015), Explaining knowledge sharing with social capital theory in information systems development projects. *Industrial Management and Data Systems*, 115(5), 883–900.

Liu, C.-H. (2013) The processes of social capital and employee creativity: Empirical evidence from intraorganizational networks. *International Journal of Human Resource Management*, 24(20), 3886–3902.

Lu, J. (2016). The performance of performance-based contracting in human services: A quasi-experiment. *Journal of Public Administration Research and Theory*, 26(2), 277–293.

McGuire, M. (2013). Network management. In M. Bevir (Ed.), *The SAGE Handbook of Governance* (pp. 436–453). London: SAGE.

Micheli, P., & Pavlov, A. (2020). What is performance measurement for? Multiple uses of performance information within organizations. *Public Administration*, 98(1), 29–45.

Miller, G. (2005). The political evolution of principal-agent models. *Annual Review of Political Science*, 8, 203–225.

Mintzberg, H. (1975). The manager's job: Folklore and fact. *Harvard Business Review*, 53(4), 49–61.

Mitchell, R., Parker, V., Giles, M., Joyce, P., & Chiang, V. (2012). Perceived value congruence and team innovation. *Journal of Occupational and Organizational Psychology*, 85(4), 626–648.

Mohammed, S., Ferzandi, L., & Hamilton, K. (2010). Metaphor no more: A 15-year review of the team mental model construct. *Journal of Management*, 36(4), 876–910.

Monnat, S. (2020). Opioid crisis in the rural U.S. In: J. Glick, S. McHale, & V. King (Eds.), *Rural families and communities in the united states: Facing challenges and leveraging opportunities* (pp. 117–143). Cham, Switzerland: Springer.

Moon, K.-K., & Christensen, R. (2020). Realizing the performance benefits of workforce diversity in the U.S. federal government: The moderating role of diversity climate. *Public Personnel Management*, 49(1), 141–165.

Moynihan, D. (2008). *The dynamics of performance management: Constructing information and reform*. Washington, DC: Georgetown University Press.

Moynihan, D. (2009). Through a glass, darkly: Understanding the effects of performance regimes. *Public Performance and Management Review*, 32(4), 592–603.

Moynihan, D. (2015). Uncovering the circumstances of performance information use: Findings from an experiment. *Public Performance and Management Review*, 39(1), 33–57.

Moynihan, D., Baekgaard, M., & Jakobsen, M. (2020). Tackling the perform-ance regime paradox: A problem-solving approach engages professional goal-based learning. *Public Administration Review*, 80(6), 1001–1010.

Moynihan, D., & Hawes, D. (2012). Responsiveness to reform values: The influence of the environment on performance information use. *Public Administration Review*, 72(s1), 95–105.

Moynihan, D., & Kroll, A. (2016). Performance management routines that work? An early assessment of the GPRA Modernization Act. *Public Administration Review*, 76(2), 314–323.

Moynihan, D., & Pandey, S. (2007). The role of organizations in fostering Public Service Motivation. *Public Administration Review*, 67(1), 40–53.

Moynihan, D., & Pandey, S. (2010). The big question for performance manage-ment: Why do managers use performance information? *Journal of Public Administration Research and Theory*, 20(4), 849–866.

Moynihan, D., Fernandez, S., Kim, S., LeRoux, K., Piotrowski, S., Wright, B., & Yang, K. (2011). Performance regimes amidst governance complexity. *Journal of Public Administration Research and Theory*, 21(issue suppl. 1), i141–i155.

Moynihan, D., Pandey, S., & Wright, B. (2012). Prosocial values and perform-ance management theory: Linking perceived social impact and performance information use. *Governance*, 25(3), 463–483.

Murthy, V. (2016). Ending the opioid epidemic: A call to action. *New England Journal of Medicine*, 375, 2413–2415.

Nahapiet, J., & Ghoshal, S. (1998). Social capital, intellectual capital, and the organizational advantage. *Academy of Management Review*, 23(2), 242–266.

National Institute on Drug Abuse [NIDA]. (2021). Opioid overdose crisis. www .drugabuse.gov/drug-topics/opioids/opioid-overdose-crisis.

Nelson, K. (2021). *Using the collective impact process as a model to address complex community problems: Lessons learned from the opioid response project*. Chapel Hill, NC: School of Government at the University of North Carolina–Chapel Hill.

Nielsen, P., & Moynihan, D. (2017). How do politicians attribute bureaucratic responsibility for performance? Negativity bias and interest group advocacy. *Journal of Public Administration Research and Theory*, 27(2), 269–283.

North, D. (1991). Institutions. *Journal of Economic Perspectives*, 5(1), 97–112.

North, D. (2008). Institutions and the performance of economies over time. In C. Menard & M. Shirley (Eds.), *Handbook of new institutional economics* (pp. 21–30). Berlin: Springer.

North Carolina Department of Health and Human Services [NCDHHS]. (2021a). Opioid action plan data dashboard. www.ncdhhs.gov/about/department-initiatives/opioid-epidemic/opioid-action-plan-data-dashboard.

North Carolina Department of Health and Human Services [NCDHHS]. (2021b). North Carolina's Opioid Action Plan. www.ncdhhs.gov/about/department-initiatives/opioid-epidemic/north-carolinas-opioid-action-plan.

Olsen, A. (2017). Human interest or hard numbers? Experiments on citizens' selection, exposure, and recall of performance information. *Public Administration Review*, 77(3), 408–420.

Ospina, S. (2016). Collective leadership and context in public administration: Bridging public leadership research and leadership studies. *Public Administration Review*, 77(2), 275–287.

Paarlberg, L., & Perry, J. (2007). Values management: Aligning employee values and organization goals. *American Review of Public Administration*, 37(4), 387–408.

Page, S. (2004). Measuring accountability for results in interagency collaboratives. *Public Administration Review*, 64(5), 591–606.

Page, S., Stone, M., Bryson, J., & Crosby, B. (2015). Public value creation by cross-sector collaborations: A framework and challenges of assessment. *Public Administration*, 93(3), 715–732.

Pasha, O., Kroll, A., & Ash, M. (2021). Assessing the equity and effectiveness of PerformanceStat systems. *Forthcoming in International Public Management Journal* (DOI: 10.1080/10967494.2021.1918300).

Pelled, L., Eisenhardt, K., & Xin, K. (1999). Exploring the black box: An analysis of work group diversity, conflict and performance. *Administrative Science Quarterly*, 44(1), 1–28.

Petersen, N. (2020). How the source of performance information matters to learning on the front-lines: Evidence from a survey experiment. *International Public Management Journal*, 23(2), 276–291.

Pfiffner, R. (2019). Why performance information use requires a managerial identity: Evidence from the field of human services. *Public Performance and Management Review*, 42(2), 405–431.

Poocharoen, O., & Wong, N. (2016). Performance management of collaborative projects: The stronger the collaboration, the less is measured. *Public Performance and Management Review*, 39(3), 607–629.

Provan, K., & Kenis, P. (2008). Modes of network governance: Structure, management, and effectiveness. *Journal of Public Administration Research and Theory*, 18 (2), 229–252.

Ryu, G. (2015). The missing link of value congruence and its consequences: The mediating role of employees' acceptance of organizational vision. *Public Personnel Management*, 44(4), 473–495.

Schein, E. (1990). Organizational culture. *American Psychologist*, 45(2), 109–119.

Schillemans, T., & Bjurstrøm, K. (2019). Trust and verification: Balancing agency and stewardship theory in the governance of agencies. *International Public Management Journal*, 23(5), 650–676.

School of Government [SOG]. (2021). The opioid response project. https://orp .sites.unc.edu/.

Seers, A. (1989). Team–member exchange quality: A new construct for role-making research. *Organizational Behavior and Human Decision Processes*, 43(1), 118–135.

Shipton, E. A., Shipton, E. E., & Shipton, A. J. (2018). A review of the opioid epidemic: What do we do about it? *Pain and Therapy*, 7, 23–36.

Siddiki, S., Kim, J., & Leach, W. (2017). Diversity, trust, and social learning in collaborative governance. *Public Administration Review*, 77(6), 863–874.

Spector, P. (1986). Perceived control by employees: A meta-analysis of studies concerning autonomy and participation at work. *Human Relations*, 39(11), 1005–1016.

Stake, R. (1995). *The art of case study research*. Thousand Oaks, CA: SAGE.

Supovitz, J., & Tognatta, N. (2013). The impact of distributed leadership on collaborative team decision making. *Leadership and Policy in Schools*, 12 (2), 101–121.

Tajfel, H., & Turner, J. (2004). An integrative theory of intergroup conflict. In: M. Hatch & M. Schultz (Eds.), *Organizational identity* (pp. 56–65). Oxford, UK: Oxford University Press.

Tantardini, M. (2019). Routine and nonroutine performance information: An assessment about substitution and complementarity. *Public Management Review*, 21(5), 755–774.

Tantardini, M., & Kroll, A. (2015). The role of organizational social capital in performance management. *Public Performance and Management Review*, 39 (1), 83–99.

U.S. Department of Health and Human Services [HHS] (2021). Opioid crisis statistics. www.hhs.gov/opioids/about-the-epidemic/opioid-crisis-statistics /index.html.

Van Dooren, W., Bouckaert, G., & Halligan, J. (2015). *Performance management in the public sector*. London: Routledge.

Van Dooren, W., & Van de Walle, S. (2008). *Performance information on the public sector: How it is used*. Basingstoke, UK: Palgrave Macmillan.

Van Slyke, D. (2007). Agents or stewards: Using theory to understand the government-nonprofit social service contracting relationship. *Journal of Public Administration Research and Theory*, 17(2), 157–187.

Wang, A.-C., Hsieh, H.-H., Tsai, C.-Y., & Cheng, B.-S. (2012). Does value congruence lead to voice? Cooperative voice and cooperative silence under team and differentiated transformational leadership. *Management and Organization Review*, 8(2), 341–370.

Wang, D., Waldman, D., & Zhang, Z. (2014). A meta-analysis of shared leadership and team effectiveness. *Journal of Applied Psychology*, 99(2), 181–198.

Watkins, D. (2013). What is organizational culture? And why should we care? *Harvard Business Review*. https://hbr.org/2013/05/what-is-organizational-culture.

Webeck, S., & Nicholson-Crotty, S. (2020). How historical and social comparisons influence interpretations of performance information. *International Public Management Journal*, 23(6), 798–821.

Willems, J. (2016). Building shared mental models of organizational effectiveness in leadership teams through team member exchange quality. *Nonprofit and Voluntary Sector Quarterly*, 45(3), 568–592.

Witesman, E., & Fernandez, S. (2013). Government contracts with private organizations: Are there differences between nonprofits and for-profits? *Nonprofit and Voluntary Sector Quarterly*, 42(4), 689–715.

Wu, Q., Cormican, K., Chen, G. (2020). A meta-analysis of shared leadership: Antecedents, consequences, and moderators. *Journal of Leadership and Organizational Studies*, 27(1), 49–64.

Yang, K., & Hsieh, J. (2007). Managerial effectiveness of government performance measurement: Testing a middle-range model. *Public Administration Review*, 67(5), 861–879.

Yin, R. (2006). Mixed methods research: Are the methods genuinely integrated or merely parallel? *Research in the Schools*, 13(1), 41–47.

Yin, R. (2013). Validity and generalization in future case study evaluations. *Evaluation*, 19(3), 321–332.

Yin, R. (2017). *Case study research and applications: Design and methods*. Thousand Oaks, CA: SAGE.

Zhang, W., Levenson, A., & Crossley, C. (2015). Move your research from the ivy tower to the board room: A primer on action research for academics, consultants, and business executives. *Human Resource Management*, 54(1), 151–174.

Zhu, J., Liao, Z., Chi, K., Yam, K., & Johnson, R. (2018). Shared leadership: A state-of-the-art review and future research agenda. *Journal of Organizational Behavior*, 39(7), 834–852.

Acknowledgments

I want to thank the University of North Carolina Chapel Hill's School of Government for providing access to the case. I am grateful to be working with Willow Jacobson and Kim Isett with whom I continue collaborating on research related to the topic of this Element. Finally, for providing comments and feedback on previous versions of this manuscript, I thank (in alphabetical order) Willow Jacobson, Donavon Johnson, Aarti Mehta-Kroll, Obed Pasha, and Travis Whetsell.

Cambridge Elements ☰

Public and Nonprofit Administration

Andrew Whitford
University of Georgia
Andrew Whitford is Alexander M. Crenshaw Professor of Public Policy in the School of Public and International Affairs at the University of Georgia. His research centers on strategy and innovation in public policy and organization studies.

Robert Christensen
Brigham Young University
Robert Christensen is professor and George Romney Research Fellow in the Marriott School at Brigham Young University. His research focuses on prosocial and antisocial behaviors and attitudes in public and nonprofit organizations.

About the Series
The foundation of this series are cutting-edge contributions on emerging topics and definitive reviews of keystone topics in public and nonprofit administration, especially those that lack longer treatment in textbook or other formats. Among keystone topics of interest for scholars and practitioners of public and nonprofit administration, it covers public management, public budgeting and finance, nonprofit studies, and the interstitial space between the public and nonprofit sectors, along with theoretical and methodological contributions, including quantitative, qualitative and mixed-methods pieces.

The Public Management Research Association
The Public Management Research Association improves public governance by advancing research on public organizations, strengthening links among interdisciplinary scholars, and furthering professional and academic opportunities in public management.

Cambridge Elements ☰

Public and Nonprofit Administration

Elements in the Series